HORTON HEARS A WHO!

By

Dr. Seuss

HarperCollins *Children's Books*

™ & © Dr. Seuss Enterprises, L.P.
All rights reserved

No part of this publication may be reproduced, stored in a retrieval system or
transmitted in any form or by any means, electronic, mechanical, photocopying,
recording or otherwise, without the prior permission of HarperCollins Publishers Ltd,
77-85 Fulham Palace Road, Hammersmith, London W6 8JB.

1 3 5 7 9 10 8 6 4 2

978-0-00-792289-5

Horton Hears a Who!
© 1954, 1982 by Dr. Seuss Enterprises, L.P.
All Rights Reserved
Published by arrangement with Random House Inc., New York, USA
First published in the UK in 1976
This edition published in the UK in 2012 by HarperCollins Children's Books, a
division of HarperCollins Publishers Ltd, 77-85 Fulham Palace Road, London W6 8JB

www.harpercollins.co.uk

Printed and bound in China

For My Great Friend,
Mitsugi Nakamura
of Kyoto,
Japan.

On the fifteenth of May, in the Jungle of Nool,
In the heat of the day, in the cool of the pool,
He was splashing...enjoying the jungle's great joys...
When Horton the elephant heard a small noise.

So Horton stopped splashing. He looked towards the sound.
"That's funny," thought Horton. "There's no one around."
Then he heard it again! Just a very faint yelp
As if some tiny person were calling for help.
"I'll help you," said Horton. "But *who* are you? *Where?*"
He looked and he looked. He could see nothing there
But a small speck of dust blowing past through the air.

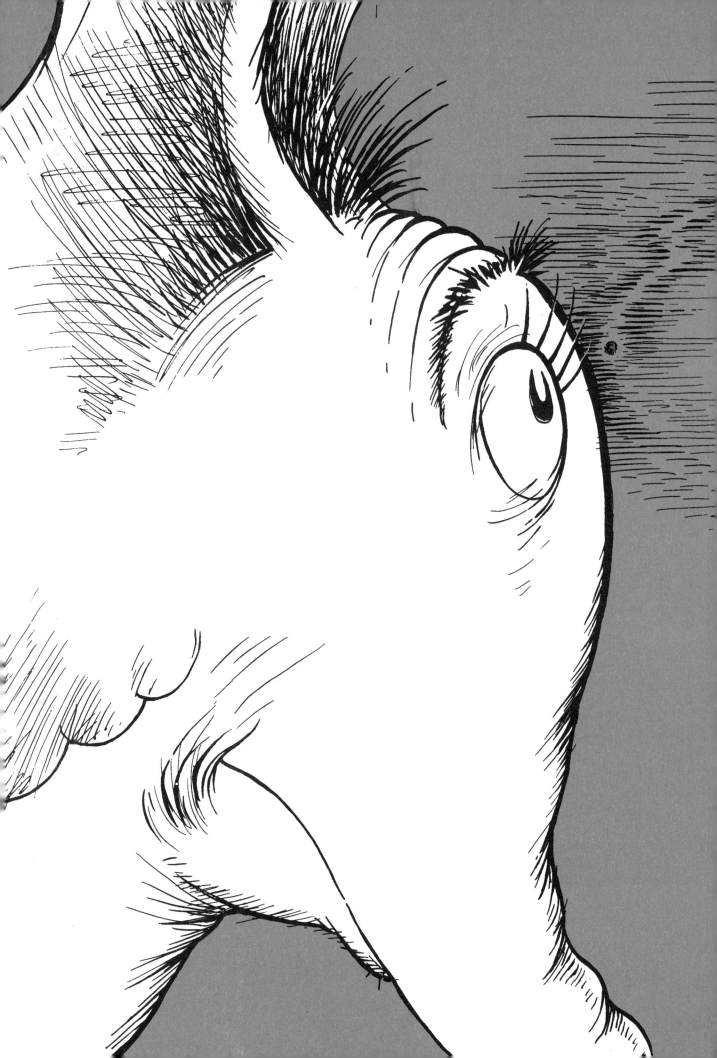

"I say!" murmured Horton. "I've never heard tell
Of a small speck of dust that is able to yell.
So you know what I think?... Why, I think that there must
Be someone on top of that small speck of dust!
Some sort of a creature of *very* small size,
Too small to be seen by an elephant's eyes...

"...some poor little person who's shaking with fear
That he'll blow in the pool! He has no way to steer!
I'll just have to save him. Because, after all,
A person's a person, no matter how small."

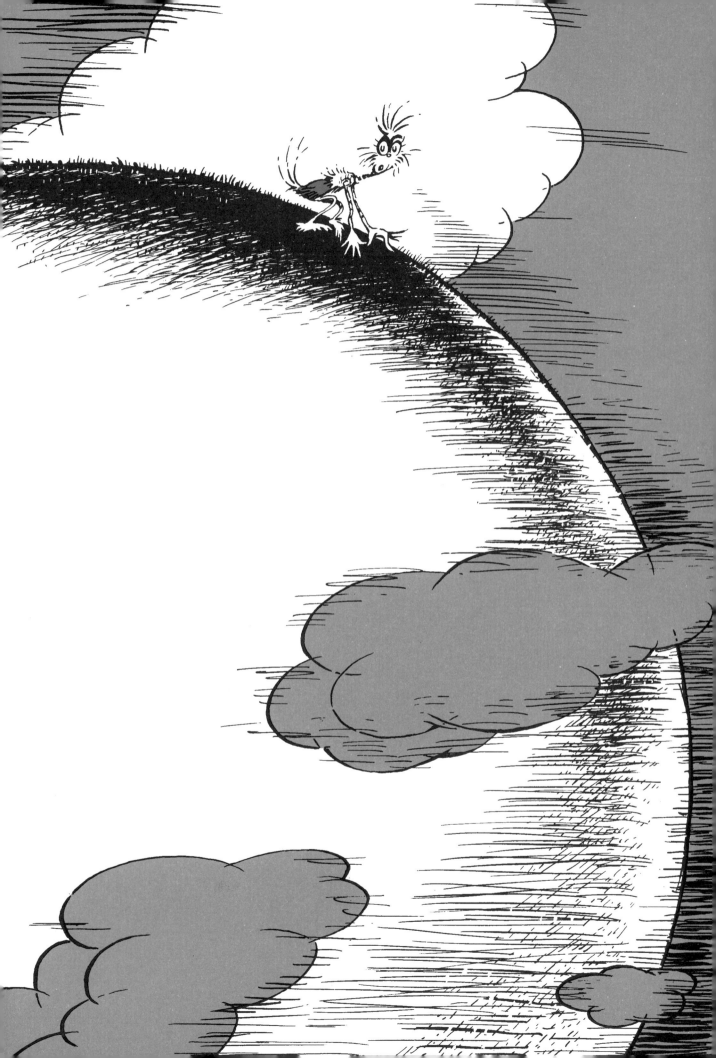

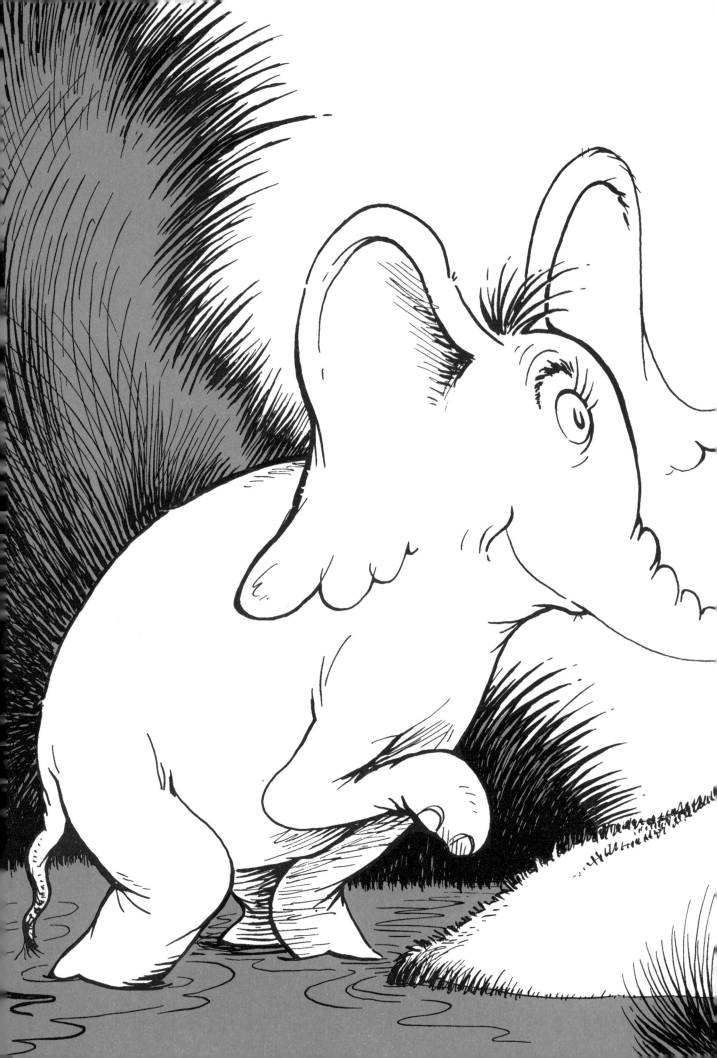

So, gently, and using the greatest of care,
The elephant stretched his great trunk through the air,
And he lifted the dust speck and carried it over
And placed it down, safe, on a very soft clover.

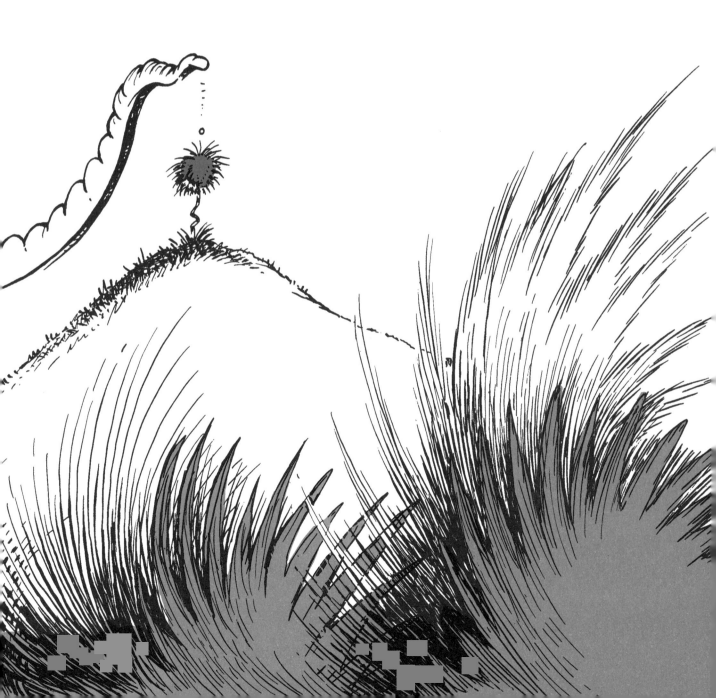

"Humpf!" humpfed a voice. 'Twas a sour kangaroo.
And the young kangaroo in her pouch said "Humpf!" too
"Why, that speck is as small as the head of a pin.
A person on *that?* . . . Why, there never has been!"

"Believe me," said Horton. "I tell you sincerely,
My ears are quite keen and I heard him quite clearly.
I *know* there's a person down there. And, what's more,
Quite likely there's two. Even three. Even four.
Quite likely . . .

" . . . a family, for all that we know!
A family with children just starting to grow.
So, please," Horton said, "as a favour to me,
Try not to disturb them. Just please let them be."

"I think you're a fool!" laughed the sour kangaroo
And the young kangaroo in her pouch said, "Me, too!
You're the biggest blame fool in the Jungle of Nool!"
And the kangaroos plunged in the cool of the pool.
"What terrible splashing!" the elephant frowned.
"I can't let my very small persons get drowned!
I've *got* to protect them. I'm bigger than they."
So he plucked up the clover and hustled away.

Through the high jungle tree tops, the news quickly spread:
"He talks to a dust speck! He's out of his head!
Just look at him walk with that speck on that flower!"
And Horton walked, worrying, almost an hour.
"Should I put this speck down?..." Horton thought with alarm.
"If I do, these small persons may come to great harm.
I *can't* put it down. And I *won't!* After all
A person's a person. No matter how small."

Then Horton stopped walking.

The speck-voice was talking!

The voice was so faint he could just barely hear it.

"Speak *up,* please," said Horton. He put his ear near it.

"My friend," came the voice, "you're a *very* fine friend.
You've helped all us folks on this dust speck no end.
You've saved all our houses, our ceilings and floors.
You've saved all our churches and grocery stores."

"You mean . . ." Horton gasped, "you have *buildings* there, *too?*"

"Oh, yes," piped the voice. "We most certainly do. . ."
"I know," called the voice, "I'm too small to be seen
But I'm Mayor of a town that is friendly and clean.
Our buildings, to you, would seem terribly small
But to us, who aren't big, they are wonderfully tall.
My town is called *Who*-ville, for I am a *Who*
And we *Whos* are all thankful and grateful to you."

And Horton called back to the Mayor of the town,
"You're safe now. Don't worry. I won't let you down."

But, just as he spoke to the Mayor of the speck,
Three big jungle monkeys climbed up Horton's neck!
The Wickersham Brothers came shouting, "What rot!
This elephant's talking to *Whos* who are *not!*
There *aren't* any *Whos!* And they *don't* have a Mayor!
And *we're* going to stop all this nonsense! *So there!*"

They snatched Horton's clover! They carried it off
To a black-bottomed eagle named Vlad Vlad-i-koff,
A mighty strong eagle, of very swift wing,
And they said, "Will you kindly get rid of this thing?"
And, before the poor elephant even could speak,
That eagle flew off with the flower in his beak.

All that late afternoon and far into the night
That black-bottomed bird flapped his wings in fast flight,
While Horton chased after, with groans, over stones
That tattered his toenails and battered his bones,
And begged, "Please don't harm all my little folks, who
Have as much right to live as us bigger folks do!"

But far, far beyond him, that eagle kept flapping
And over his shoulder called back, "Quit your yapping.
I'll fly the night through. I'm a bird. I don't mind it.
And I'll hide this, tomorrow, where *you'll* never find it!"

And at 6:56 the next morning he did it.
It sure was a terrible place that he hid it.
He let that small clover drop somewhere inside
Of a great patch of clovers a hundred miles wide!
"Find THAT!" sneered the bird. "But I think you will fail."
And he left
With a flip
Of his black-bottomed tail.

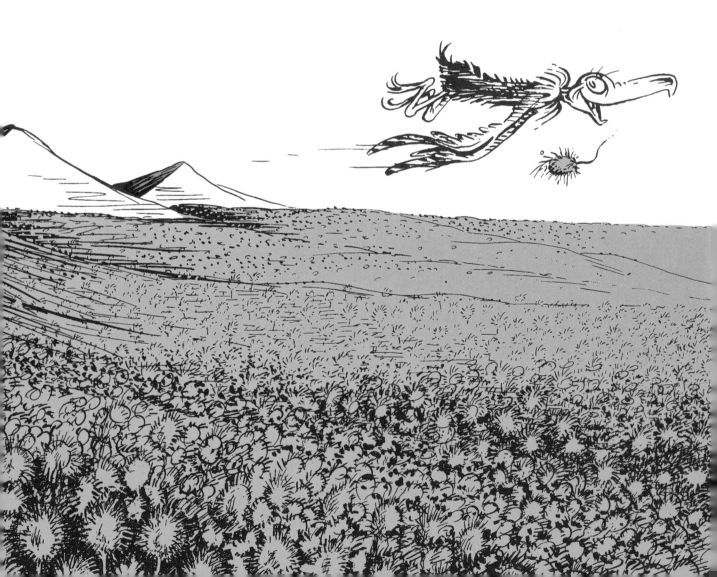

"I'll find it!" cried Horton. "I'll find it or bust!
I SHALL find my friends on my small speck of dust!"
And clover, by clover, by clover with care
He picked up and searched them, and called, "Are you there?"
But clover, by clover, by clover he found
That the one that he sought for was just not around.
And by noon poor old Horton, more dead than alive,
Had picked, searched, and piled up, nine thousand and five.

Then, on through the afternoon, hour after hour...
Till he found them at last! On the three millionth flower!
"My friends!" cried the elephant. "Tell me! Do tell!
Are you safe? Are you sound? Are you whole? Are you well?"

From down on the speck came the voice of the Mayor:

"We've *really* had trouble! Much more than our share.
When that black-bottomed birdie let go and we dropped,
We landed so hard that our clocks have all stopped.
Our tea-pots are broken. Our rocking-chairs smashed.
And our bicycle tyres all blew up when we crashed.
So, Horton, *please!*" pleaded that voice of the Mayor's,
"Will you stick by us *Whos* while we're making repairs?"

"Of course," Horton answered. "Of course I will stick.
I'll stick by you small folks through thin and through thick!"

"Humpf!"
Humpfed a voice!
"For almost two days you've run wild and insisted
On chatting with persons who've never existed.
Such carryings-on in our peaceable jungle!
We've had quite enough of your bellowing bungle!
And I'm here to state," snapped the big kangaroo,
"That your silly nonsensical game is all through!"
And the young kangaroo in her pouch said, "Me, too!"

"With the help of the Wickersham Brothers and dozens
Of Wickersham Uncles and Wickersham Cousins
And Wickersham In-Laws, whose help I've engaged,
You're going to be roped! And you're going to be caged!
And, as for your dust speck...hah! *That* we shall boil
In a hot steaming kettle of Beezle-Nut oil!"

"*Boil* it?..." gasped Horton!
"Oh, that you *can't* do!
It's all full of persons!
They'll *prove* it to you!"

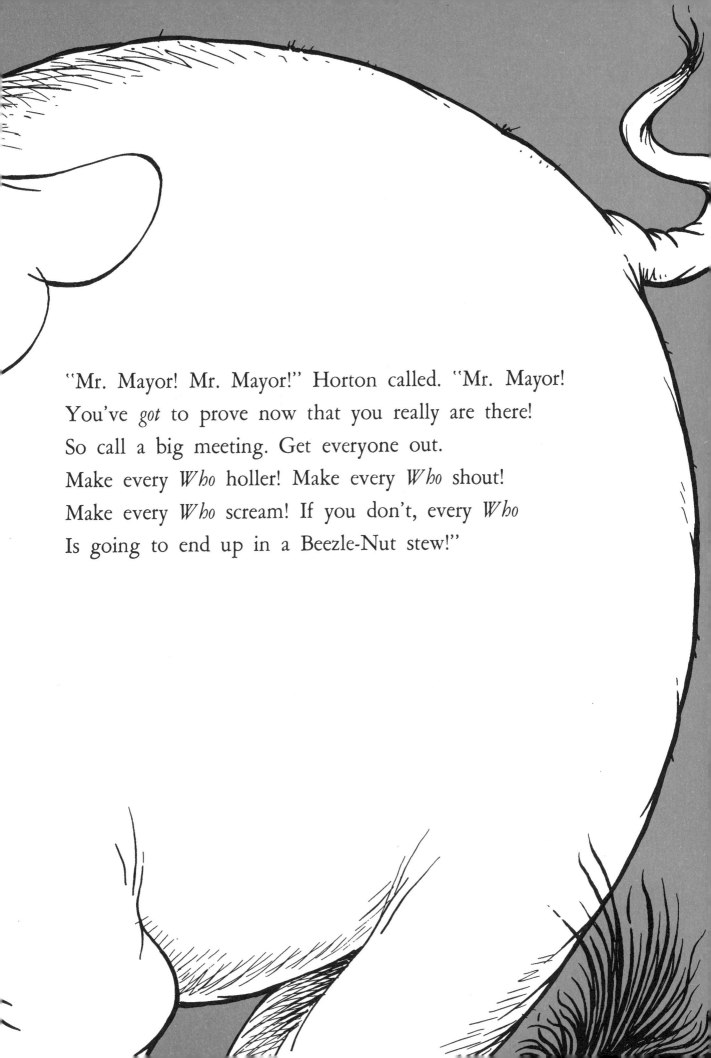

"Mr. Mayor! Mr. Mayor!" Horton called. "Mr. Mayor!
You've *got* to prove now that you really are there!
So call a big meeting. Get everyone out.
Make every *Who* holler! Make every *Who* shout!
Make every *Who* scream! If you don't, every *Who*
Is going to end up in a Beezle-Nut stew!"

And, down on the dust speck, the scared little Mayor
Quick called a big meeting in *Who*-ville Town Square.
And his people cried loudly. They cried out in fear:
"We are here! We are here! We are here! We are here!"

The elephant smiled: "That was clear as a bell.
You kangaroos surely heard *that* very well."
"All I heard," snapped the big kangaroo, "was the breeze,
And the faint sound of wind through the far-distant trees.
I heard no small voices. And you didn't either."
And the young kangaroo in her pouch said, "Me, neither."

"Grab him!" they shouted. "And cage the big dope!
Lasso his stomach with ten miles of rope!
Tie the knots tight so he'll *never* shake loose!
Then dunk that dumb speck in the Beezle-Nut juice!"

Horton fought back with great vigour and vim
But the Wickersham gang was too many for him.
They beat him! They mauled him! They started to haul
Him into his cage! But he managed to call
To the Mayor: "Don't give up! I believe in you all!
A person's a person, no matter how small!
And you very small persons will *not* have to die
If you make yourselves heard! *So come on, now, and TRY!*"

The Mayor grabbed a tom-tom. He started to smack it.
And, all over *Who*-ville, they whooped up a racket.
They rattled tin kettles! They beat on brass pans,
On garbage pail tops and old cranberry cans!
They blew on bazookas and blasted great toots
On clarinets, oom-pahs and boom-pahs and flutes!

Great gusts of loud racket rang high through the air.
They rattled and shook the whole sky! And the Mayor
Called up through the howling mad hullabaloo:
"Hey, Horton! *How's this?* Is our sound coming through?"

And Horton called back, "I can hear you just fine.
But the kangaroos' ears aren't as strong, quite, as mine.
They don't hear a thing! Are you *sure* all your boys
Are doing their best? Are they ALL making noise?
Are you sure every *Who* down in *Who*-ville is working?
Quick! Look through your town! Is there anyone shirking?"

Through the town rushed the Mayor, from the east to the west.
But *every*one seemed to be doing his best.
*Every*one seemed to be yapping or yipping!
*Every*one seemed to be beeping or bipping!
But it *wasn't enough,* all this ruckus and roar!
He HAD to find someone to help him make more.
He raced through each building! He searched floor-to-floor!

And, just as he felt he was getting nowhere,
And almost about to give up in despair,
He suddenly burst through a door and that Mayor
Discovered one shirker! Quite hidden away
In the Fairfax Apartments (Apartment 12-J)
A very small, *very* small shirker named Jo-Jo
Was standing, just standing, and bouncing a Yo-Yo!
Not making a sound! Not a yipp! Not a chirp!
And the Mayor rushed inside and he grabbed the young twerp!

And he climbed with the lad up the Eiffelberg Tower.

"This," cried the Mayor, "is your town's darkest hour!
The time for all *Whos* who have blood that is red
To come to the aid of their country!" he said.
"We've GOT to make noises in greater amounts!
So, open your mouth, lad! For every voice counts!"

Thus he spoke as he climbed. When they got to the top,
The lad cleared his throat and he shouted out, "YOPP!"

And that Yopp...

That one small, extra Yopp put it over!

Finally, at last! From that speck on that clover

Their voices were heard! They rang out clear and clean.

And the elephant smiled. "Do you see what I mean?...

They've proved they ARE persons, no matter how small.

And their whole world was saved by the Smallest of All!"

"How true! Yes, how true," said the big kangaroo.

"And, from now on, you know what I'm planning to do?...

From now on, I'm going to protect them with you!"

And the young kangaroo in her pouch said,...

"...ME, TOO!
From sun in the summer. From rain when it's fall-ish,
I'm going to protect them. No matter how small-ish!"

1

On Selecting Heroes

The dictionary defines *hero* as "a person admired for his or her achievements and noble qualities; one who displays courage." That definition seems straightforward enough. But in going from the abstract to the concrete—that is, in saying a particular person does or does not qualify as a hero—a measure of subjectivity inevitably comes into play. Heroism is, to a great extent, in the eye of the beholder. While one observer might focus on an individual's achievements, another might focus on the individual's mistakes and setbacks. Where one observer sees evidence of a noble quality, another may discern faults or a baseness of character. It cannot even be said that courage means the same thing to everyone: one person's courage is another's foolhardiness or fanaticism.

If obtaining agreement on who should or should not be considered a hero is always somewhat elusive, selecting a small group of heroes representative of a major nation or culture or religion is an

Opposite: The purpose of this book is to introduce readers to various aspects of Islamic history and civilization through brief biographies of important figures. The book by no means constitutes a comprehensive list of Islamic heroes, but it can serve as a starting point for further research.

The American civil rights leader Malcolm X is a hero to many Muslims, who admire him for publicizing orthodox Islam in the United States and fighting for social justice.

especially daunting task. The difficulties of picking just a few heroes of Islam for inclusion in this book should be readily apparent. After all, Islamic civilization has a history that extends back more than 1,400 years. And today over 50 countries have Muslim-majority populations, to say nothing of the large number of countries with significant Muslim minorities, including Russia, India, China, and several European nations. Geographically, the Islamic world spans the globe from Morocco to Indonesia, and Islam claims nearly 2 billion adherents in all. Perhaps no other religion can claim such geographical and cultural diversity.

It should also be noted that modern Muslims, like adherents of other faiths, vary in their level of religious commitment, and in the way they interpret some of their religion's tenets and traditions. Thus an ideologically secular Muslim and a traditional, devout Muslim would probably list different figures from Islamic history as heroes. The same might be expected from a more liberal Muslim and a member of the fundamentalist Wahhabi sect.

 Words to Understand in This Chapter

caliph—a successor of the prophet Muhammad as leader of the Islamic community.

mausoleum—a large, usually stone building where the dead are entombed above ground.

Shiite—a follower of Shiism, Islam's second-largest sect worldwide.

Sufi—a practitioner of Sufism, a Muslim mystical tradition.

In addition, other than the three places that all Muslims universally acknowledge as holy—Mecca, Madina, and Jerusalem—there exist a large number of local shrines scattered throughout the Islamic world. Some of these shrines are particularly important to **Shiite** Muslims, while others are memorials to **Sufi** heroes, such as the **mausoleum** of Jalal al-Din al-Rumi in Turkey, Ibn al-'Arabi in Syria, or Khawaja Moeenuddin al-Chishti in Pakistan.

A Wide Range of Heroes

This book is by no means intended to be comprehensive; a volume of this length could never begin to touch on the many significant figures in the long and rich history of Islam. Rather, the goal of this book is to introduce readers—through biographies of a handful of people whom most educated Muslims would respect or consider important in the history and development of Islam—to various currents in, and aspects of, Islamic history and civilization. The heroes selected for inclusion in this book span the history of Islam, from its seventh-century beginnings to the late 20th century. They represent various ethnic and cultural groups, reflecting the diversity of the Muslim community of believers. And they played a range of roles, from messenger to military leader to mystic.

The book begins with the prophet Muhammad, the central human figure of Islam. Other individuals featured include Ali, one of Muhammad's relatives and closest companions and the fourth **caliph**; Rabia al-Adawiyya, a female Sufi master of the eighth century; the 12th-century Kurdish political and military leader Salah al-Din (known in the West as Saladin); Malcolm X, perhaps the best-known American Muslim; and Zainab al-Ghazali, founder of the Muslim Women's Association. The final chapter focuses on the holiest cities of Islam, including Mecca, Madina, and Jerusalem, and explains why these places are revered by Muslims.

In addition to the figures profiled in this volume, there are many other individuals whom Muslims would identify as heroes. Asian Muslims might list such people as Shah Waliullah, the preeminent reformer and leader of the 18th-century Muslim intellectual revival; Tipu Sultan, one of the last Indian rulers to resist Britain's colonialist advance; or Muhammad Iqbal, a poet and intellectual of the early 20th century. Turks might feel that important sultans of the Ottoman Empire, such as Murad I, Suleiman the Magnificent, or Mehmet al-Fatih, should be included because of the large role they play in the Muslim historical imagination. Individuals such as 'Urabi, 'Abd al-Qasim al-Jaza'iri, Sulayman al-Halabi, or Muhammad 'Abdu might be among those who are remembered as heroes by Arab Muslims. Americans may consider people like boxer Muhammad Ali or basketball star Kareem Abdul Jabbar as heroes; both men have been activists for Muslim causes around the world during and after their sports careers. Or people like Keith Ellison, the first Muslim American elected to the U.S. Congress.

Although several women are included in this book, many other women have played important roles in the history and development of Islam. One of these was the prophet Muhammad's wife Ayesha. After Muhammad's death she became a political leader in her own right, leading a rebellion against the fourth caliph because of a disagreement over state policy. After losing her attempt to lead the Muslim community, she retired to a life of teaching and became an important part of the developing Islamic legal tradition. Ayesha played a significant role in establishing the foundational opinions of Islamic law and narrated a large number of pivotal statements about the Prophet.

Another significant figure in the growth and development of Islamic law was the jurist, theologian, and mystic Abu Hamid al-Ghazali (1058–1111). Al-Ghazali had a huge impact on the interpretation and development of Islam. His own life story is quite fascinating: after acquiring an important position at one of the most prominent universities of the time, al-Ghazali suddenly quit, impelled by his desire to discover spiritual truth. He spent the next 10 years anonymously wandering around the Muslim world, seeking knowledge and truth from different contemporary masters. He returned to his position and wrote the hugely influential book *The Revival of the Religious Sciences* as well as the famous *The Incoherence of the Philosophers*. Later in his life al-Ghazali turned to Sufism as a spiritual method and discipline. His influential teachings helped Sufism become accepted into Islamic theology.

Other prominent Muslim philosopher-scholars include al-Kindi (ca. 800–873); al-Farabi (870?–950); Avicenna, known also as Ibn Sina (980–1037); Averroës, known also as Ibn Rushd (1126–1198); Ibn Taymiyya (1263–1328); and Ibn Khaldun (1332–1406?).

In addition to Muhammad and Ali, there are many other figures from the early years of Islam whose stories are important and whom many Muslims consider heroes. The lives of Muhammad's companions, especially the first three caliphs, are fascinating. Many other leaders are also remembered fondly. For example, Umar ibn 'Abd al-Aziz, caliph from 717 to 720, was so famed for his justice and compassion that some consider him the fifth "rightly guided" caliph.

The point is that throughout the history of Islam there have been many rulers, scientists, artists, and scholars who are widely remembered, respected, and honored for their spectacular achievements. The stories selected for this book provide some basic information about important Muslim figures and are intended as a starting point for more in-depth research into the world of Islam.

 # Text-Dependent Questions

1. Who are some contemporary Americans that Muslims may consider to be heroes?
2. What Medieval Muslim played a significant role in the growth and development of Islamic law?

 # Research Project

Choose one of the people who are mentioned in this chapter as Muslim heroes, yet are not profiled in chapters two through seven of this book. Using your school library or the Internet, find out more about this person's life and accomplishments. Write a two-page report that presents these accomplishments to the class, and explains why Muslims might consider this person to be a hero.

2

The Prophet Muhammad

In the year 610 CE, during Ramadan (the ninth month of the lunar calendar used by Arabs at the time), a man named Muhammad ibn Abd Allah left his home in the oasis city of Makka (better known as Mecca), on the Arabian Peninsula, and made his way north to Mount Hira. There was a cave on the mountain where Muhammad retreated every year to pray and meditate.

At this time, some people on the Arabian Peninsula followed *monotheistic* religions, such as Judaism, Christianity, and Zoroastrianism. Most Arabs, however, were polytheists who believed in many gods and goddesses. The Arabs asked their deities for guidance on all kinds of matters, from marriage arrangements to the mediation of disagreements. In addition to the various minor deities, some Arabs believed in a supreme, impersonal god known as Allah ("The God"—*Allah* is the Arabic word for "God"). Allah was thought to provide rain, and His name was invoked to seal agreements between tribes and individuals, but beyond this He was prayed

Opposite: A view of the Prophet's Mosque in Madina, Saudi Arabia. It is here that Muhammad, Islam's most important messenger and most revered leader, is buried.

to no more often than the lesser gods and goddesses.

Muhammad's home city, Mecca, was the location of an ancient shrine known as the Kaaba. This square building (the word *kaaba* means "cube" in Arabic) was a holy place believed to have been built by Adam, the first man, as a place of worship, and later rebuilt by the prophet Abraham and his son Ishmael. In Muhammad's day, Arabs could worship all their gods and goddesses at this holy place. Mecca, therefore, was the destination of a huge annual pilgrimage. The tribes living in Mecca grew wealthy through trade with the pilgrims who came to visit the Kaaba because of its religious significance.

Muhammad was upset that many Meccans had become greedy and no longer took care of poor members of their community, which had once been a tradition among Arab tribes. There were other cruel aspects of Arab culture that distressed him. Women were oppressed; they were denied the right to inherit property and had no rights if they were divorced. Muhammad also disagreed with the practice of polytheism; he worshiped only Allah.

On the 27th night of Ramadan, while Muhammad was sleeping in the cave on Mount Hira, the archangel Gabriel appeared to him and told Muhammad that he was to be the messenger of Allah. The visitation of Gabriel would later be recorded in the Qur'an, the holy book of Islam, in sura (chapter) 96, verses 1–5:

> Read! In the name of your Lord, Who created, created man, out of a (mere) clot of congealed blood. Read! And your Lord is Most Bountiful, He Who taught by the Pen, taught man that which he knew not.

Muhammad listened to the words of God, as given to him by the archangel Gabriel, and soon began to preach this message to

 # Words to Understand in This Chapter

martyr—a person who chooses to die rather than give up his or her religious beliefs.
monotheistic—relating to the belief in one Supreme God.

This miniature painting depicts Abraham's attempt to obey God's command and sacrifice his son; the angel pictured at the right is carrying a sheep for him to sacrifice instead. Abraham, who lived around 1900 BCE, is an important figure in the development of monotheism and is considered an ancestor of the Arabs.

the people of Mecca. The key element of the message is that there is only one God, Allah, and that Muslims must submit themselves to His will. The teachings of Muhammad evolved into a religion that became known as Islam, a word derived from the Arabic verb *aslama*, which means "submitted." A Muslim, or follower of Islam, is someone who submits himself or herself to the will of God.

The Early Life of Muhammad

The precise date of Muhammad's birth is not known, but most historians believe he was born around the year 570 CE, in Mecca. His father, a merchant named Abd Allah ibn al-Muttalib, died before the boy's birth. When Muhammad was about six years old, his mother, Amina bint Wahb, took him to visit relatives in Yathrib, an oasis community about 200 miles north of Mecca. She died on the return journey.

Muhammad's grandfather, Abd al-Muttalib, then took over his care. Muhammad probably learned something of leadership from his grandfather, as Abd al-Muttalib was a powerful political leader in Mecca and often presided over the city's council of elders. However, Abd al-Muttalib died when the boy was eight years old.

After this, Muhammad's uncle, an influential Meccan merchant named Abu Talib, raised him into adulthood.

Muhammad was a member of the Hashim (Hashimite) clan, part of the powerful Quraysh tribe, which had become rich through trade. At this time on the Arabian Peninsula, the tribe was the main unit of social organization. Each tribe included several clans—smaller groupings of related families. Preservation of the tribe and clan was an important value in Arabian society. Belonging to a tribe also provided protection; though vendettas were common, the threat of intertribal bloodshed helped hold together a society without a single government or set of laws.

As a child, Muhammad had to help the family by taking care of sheep. He was not able to attend school, and therefore he never learned how to read or write. As a young man, he worked for his uncle on caravans following the trade routes between Arabia and Syria. During this time, he was exposed to people of many cultures and religious backgrounds.

A photograph of a contemporary Bedouin camp. In Muhammad's time many people living on the Arabian Peninsula were nomadic herders, and the ties of clan and tribe were very strong.

As a young man Muhammad worked on caravan routes between Mecca and Syria. This exposed him to a variety of cultural and religious practices.

Muhammad attracted the attention of a wealthy widow, Khadija, after he agreed to sell some of her goods in Syria. Khadija was pleased when Muhammad sold her goods for a large profit, and as she got to know him she was impressed with Muhammad's honesty and character. In time, Khadija proposed to Muhammad, and he agreed to the marriage even though she was 15 years older. Muhammad and Khadija eventually had four daughters, as well as two sons who died in childhood.

As Muhammad grew older, he became widely respected as a wise and honest man. His cousin Ali ibn Abi Talib once described the middle-aged Muhammad as follows: "[Muhammad was] of middle stature, neither tall nor short. His complexion was rosy white; his eyes black; his hair, thick, brilliant, and beautiful, fell to his shoulders. His profuse beard fell to his breast. . . . There was such sweetness in his visage that no one, once in his presence, could leave him. If I hungered, a single look at the Prophet's face dispelled the hunger."

The Early Days of Islam

Soon after he received the first revelation in the cave on Mount Hira, Muhammad began to preach about the oneness of God and

His plan for creation, sharing this message first with family members and friends. The first convert to Islam was Muhammad's wife, Khadija. The next followers to be converted were his cousin Ali; a servant, Zaid; and a kinsman, Abu Bakr, who held a high rank in the Quraysh tribe. Abu Bakr was an influential man; he soon brought five others into the new faith. These men would come to be known as "the Companions" and would remain with Muhammad throughout the rest of his life.

After the first message from Gabriel in the cave on Mount Hira, Muhammad continued to receive messages from God throughout the rest of his life. These messages would eventually be recorded in the Qur'an, the holy scriptures of Islam. The Qur'an is primarily a book of moral and ethical guidance for the individual and the community.

The exact nature of the way the Qur'anic revelations came to Muhammad is the subject of much debate in Islamic history. Most Muslims believe that Gabriel came from heaven with the revelation from God and recited the verses to Muhammad. Only Muhammad could see Gabriel, and after the archangel left, Muhammad would recite the verses he received to his companions. The Prophet also designated scribes to write down the verses on whatever material was available at the time. Some verses were preserved through memorization, others written on scraps of leather, flat stone tablets, and pieces of camel bone. An authoritative text of the Qur'an that contained all of the revelations would not be compiled until some years after Muhammad's death.

Between 610 and 613, Muhammad preached God's message mostly in secret, afraid that the small Muslim community would not be able to defend itself from persecution at the hands of the polytheistic Meccans. During this time, the Prophet gained many converts to the faith.

With this growth in the Muslim community's numbers, the faith began to be preached openly and publicly. Muslims began to intercept pilgrims on their way to Mecca, imploring them to recognize Allah as the one true God. Muhammad also called on people to stop oppressing the poor, to give money in charity, and to stop certain morally horrendous practices, such as burying a newborn infant alive just because the child was a girl. The message of Islam, therefore, was more than just theological truth; it was also a message of social revival and reform.

Muhammad was a persuasive, charismatic speaker, and this helped him to win many converts. Perhaps even more influential was the beauty of his character. For example, even though leaders of the Quraysh tribe came to see Muhammad as an enemy, they also recognized that he was one of the most noble and trustworthy persons among them. The eloquence of the Qur'anic revelations, and the message of social justice that Islam presented, was also attractive to many people.

The Qur'an contains God's revelations to Muhammad and is the holiest scripture of Islam.

Persecution of the Muslims

At first, the Quraysh leaders tolerated Muhammad, but they soon grew fearful of his influence. They could do nothing about free men who pledged themselves to Islam, but the Quraysh acted with brutality toward slaves who accepted Allah; the hapless slaves were relentlessly tortured and forced to recant. Abu Bakr, who was quite wealthy, used much of his personal fortune to buy freedom for the tortured slaves, who upon their release joined the Muslim community. In 616 a powerful Quraysh leader named Umar ibn al-Khattab became a Muslim and brought many followers with him to Islam, signaling an even higher public profile for the new faith.

The Quraysh leaders were wealthy and influential, and they believed that the Islamic message of monotheism and social justice threatened their position. If people converted to Islam, they would stop traveling to Mecca to worship their idols, which would affect the livelihoods of many people who had grown rich through trade with pilgrims. In addition, an important part of Muhammad's teaching was that the rich should share their wealth with members of the community who were less fortunate. This idea was not particularly popular among the wealthy members of the Quraysh tribe.

To curb the growing influence of Muhammad and his followers, the Quraysh commenced a systematic and official persecution of Muslims. They passed laws prohibiting all business and social relations between Muslims and non-Muslims. The boycott of Muslims was so intense that many Muslims could not earn a living, and some even starved to death. The homes and properties of Muslims were confiscated or looted. At the same time, the Meccans targeted and tortured Muslims, especially those who were poor and powerless. A man named Abu Yasir and his wife, Umm Yasir, were killed because of their faith, becoming the first *martyrs* of Islam. Others, including Muhammad, were physically assaulted. Tribal leaders even plotted to kill Muhammad and his prominent followers, but this plot failed. Ultimately, however, this oppression forced the Muslims to begin looking for a new home outside Mecca.

This time of suffering and oppression was made even more difficult for Muhammad by the death of Khadija in 619. That same year, Muhammad's uncle, Abu Talib, also died. Abu Talib had been both a close friend and a powerful protector. After his death, Muhammad could no longer remain in Mecca.

In 620 representatives from Yathrib invited Muhammad to come to their city and mediate disputes between two warring tribes. Over a period of several months during 621 and 622, small groups of Muslims secretly left Mecca and traveled to Yathrib. Muhammad was among the last of the approximately 200 Muslims to leave Mecca; he waited to ensure that the persecuted Muslims would reach Yathrib before he left. It took many days for

After the Muslim community moved from Mecca to Yathrib in 622 CE, the first mosque was built and the first Islamic government established. This is a contemporary view of the Prophet's Mosque in Madina, which covers an area that is roughly as large as the entire city of Yathrib in Muhammad's time.

Muhammad to arrive at Yathrib because he was forced to hide from assassins dispatched by the Quraysh. On September 24, 622, Muhammad arrived at the city's gates, where he was welcomed by his followers. This migration is a central event in the early history of Islam; it is known as the *Hijra*, from an Arabic word meaning to migrate or to leave one's tribe.

The *Hijra* was significant in part because by leaving Mecca, the Muslims had rejected the Arab tradition of tribe and clan. The Meccans vowed to destroy the Muslims who had left. For their part, the people of Yathrib recognized that the migration of the Muslims meant certain warfare with Mecca. Thus, by accepting Muhammad and the migrant

This view of the Battle of Badr illustrated a 16th-century Ottoman manuscript. Muhammad proved to be a brave leader and an inspired military strategist in battles with the Quraysh and other opponents of Islam.

Muslims, Yathrib was making an enormous political and ethical commitment. (The city would eventually be renamed Madinat al-Nabi, or "City of the Prophet"; it is better known today as Madina or, particularly in the West, as Medina.) Many of the people of Madina accepted Islam, and Muhammad soon established the first Islamic government there. From Madina, Muhammad directed the spread of the Muslim community in other parts of Arabia.

War Between the Meccans and Muslims

The Muslims knew that they would have to fight the Meccans at some point. For protection, Muhammad concluded a treaty with the various tribal groups in Madina. The gist of the agreement, which was known as *wathiqat al-Madina*, was mutual cooperation in defense of the city in case of an attack, and an outlining of a procedure for prosecuting crimes committed by a member of one tribe or community against a person of a different community.

In 624, when Muhammad was about 53 years old, he led a Muslim army of 300 soldiers that fought with a Quraysh army at a dry riverbed known as Wadi Badr, located about 20 miles south of Madina. The Muslims were outnumbered by three to one, yet they fought bravely and defeated the larger Quraysh force. The Battle of Badr was the first significant military victory won by the Muslims.

The victory was important, but the Quraysh remained a serious threat. The following year, Abu Sufyan, a powerful Quraysh leader, led an army of 3,000 warriors against Muhammad and his followers at Uhud, just north of Madina. The Muslims were routed in the battle, and Muhammad was carried off the field suffering grave wounds. Abu Sufyan believed Muhammad had been killed, and he returned to Mecca to spread the news. But Muhammad was not dead, and he recovered from his wounds.

Soon after this setback, Muhammad led an attack on the Banu Qaynuqa', a Jewish tribe in Madina. Not only had the Banu Qaynuqa' broken the *wathiqat al-Madina*, refusing to come to the defense of the Muslims as the treaty required, but they were also suspected of providing information about the Muslims' movements to the attacking Quraysh. After a quarrel in the market led to bloodshed, the Banu Qaynuqa' gathered an army of 700 men, asked allied tribes for reinforcements, and retired to fortified castles on the outskirts of Madina. At this the Prophet quickly gathered a force and laid siege to the fortresses of the Banu Qaynuqa', demanding an unconditional surrender. When their anticipated reinforcements failed to materialize, the Banu Qaynuqa' were forced to surrender in 626. The Prophet ordered them to leave the city and its vicinity without their possessions.

In 627 Abu Sufyan again led a large army against Muhammad and his followers. This time, the Meccans numbered more than 10,000. When Muhammad heard about the advancing army, he knew that he would not be able to raise an army that could match the attacking force. Instead, he defended Madina by having a deep trench dug around the part of the city that was not protected by walls or natural barriers. The trench, and Muslim archers on the other side, would prevent the enemy cavalry from entering the city. The Muslims had only a week to prepare for the attack, but they managed to complete the trench in six days.

Abu Sufyan was upset when he arrived at Madina and found the defenses in place. The Meccans had expected to gain a quick victory by storming the city with their cavalry. They had not brought enough food or supplies for a protracted siege, and there was not much food available outside the city. The Meccans made several attacks, but the defenders were able to repel each one.

According to reports from the time, a leader of the banished Banu Qaynuqa' tribe, which had sided with the Meccans during this attack, contacted the leader of another Jewish tribe still in Madina, the Banu Qurayza, and convinced him to break the agreement with the Muslims and allow the Meccans to enter the city. This could have doomed the Muslim community, but the Meccans and Banu Qurayza could not agree on the time for the attack. While the two groups were still arguing, the weather changed suddenly. Disheartened, the Meccans decided to give up their 20-day-long attempt to capture the city.

After the Quraysh and their allies returned to Mecca, Muhammad and his followers turned against the traitorous Banu Qurayza. Traditionally, it is believed that the men of the Banu Qurayza were executed, while the women and children became slaves. However, several medieval sources state that the Prophet merely expelled the tribe from the vicinity of Madina after defeating them in battle. According to these sources, the stories of executions and enslavement were fabrications by historical narrators who either wanted to boast about Muslim power or were hostile to the Prophet's message. (Interestingly, some stories indicate that the judgment of the Banu Qurayza was based on laws from the Jewish Torah, specifically Deuteronomy 20: 12–14.)

In 628 Muhammad and his followers decided to travel to Mecca and assert their right to worship at the Kaaba like other Arabs. The large number of Muslims who went with Muhammad to Mecca wore the clothing of pilgrims, rather than military garb, and they carried only light weapons for hunting and defense, rather than battle gear, in order to emphasize that their intention was not hostile. These Muslims were stopped by a Meccan army, which refused to allow them to continue their pilgrimage. However, the Meccans promised to let the Muslims visit the Kaaba the next year if Muhammad signed a peace agreement. Despite some opposition among his followers, Muhammad agreed to enter into a 10-year nonaggression treaty with the Meccans.

In 629 the Muslims made a pilgrimage to Mecca. During this time Meccan leaders ordered all of the city's inhabitants to stay home and lock their doors; according to early Muslim sources, Mecca seemed deserted during their pilgrimage. The Meccan leaders feared that contact with the Muslim pilgrims would lead some Meccans to convert.

When the Meccans breached the treaty later in 629, Muhammad raised an army to invade Mecca. By the time Muhammad's forces arrived at the city in January 630, however, Mecca's inhabitants had lost the will to resist. The city surrendered without a fight, and soon afterward most Meccans converted to Islam and accepted Muhammad as their leader.

The Prophet's Final Years

Even though the Meccans had persecuted Muhammad, tortured his followers, and forced him from his home, Muhammad declared a general amnesty for all people in the city. However, he did order

A modern-day Muslim pilgrim prays in Mecca. During Muhammad's time, the Kaaba (the dark square building at the center of this photo) was the site of an annual pilgrimage by the Arab tribes. In 628 Muhammad signed a treaty that would allow the Muslims to make the pilgrimage. When the Meccans breached the treaty the next year, Muhammad led an army to Mecca and forced the city to surrender.

that the stone idols be taken out of the Kaaba, and the building itself remains a revered symbol of Islam. The city of Mecca was proclaimed the Holy City of Islam, and Muhammad decreed that no unbeliever should ever be allowed to set foot inside its walls. Today, non-Muslims are still barred from Mecca.

For the remaining years of his life, Muhammad served as the religious and political leader of the Muslims. He ruled from Madina, where he conducted foreign policy with neighboring powers such as the Persian and Byzantine empires. He also oversaw the spread of Islam into much of the Arabian Peninsula through treaties, trade, and warfare.

Unlike other rulers, however, Muhammad lived modestly. He was not above mending his own clothes, milking the goats, kindling the fire, or shopping in the public market. He enjoyed dates, barley bread, milk, and honey. His wives lived in small and simply furnished apartments, and Muhammad himself kept no permanent apartment.

In March of 632 Muhammad traveled to Mecca on pilgrimage, accompanied by thousands of Muslims. After returning to Madina, he was plagued by high fevers. Muhammad died on June 8, 632, aged about 63. His body was buried in the mosque in Madina.

The Significance of Muhammad

To Muslims, Muhammad is more than just a hero—he is the most revered human figure in Islam, God's final messenger. Muslims believe that God designated both prophets and messengers to bear His divine message to humans. The message of a prophet was meant for a specific community of people, whereas that of a messenger is universal. All messengers are prophets, but not all prophets are messengers. Some people Muslims consider messen-

Leabharlanna Poiblí Chathair Baile Átha Cliath
Dublin City Public Libraries

A pre-Islamic white alabaster idol. When the Muslims took over Mecca, Muhammad and his followers destroyed all of the idols within the Kaaba.

gers whose names would also be familiar to Jews and Christians include Noah, Abraham, Moses, John the Baptist, and Jesus. Muslims believe Muhammad was the greatest and last prophet and messenger; although the message Muhammad delivered is universal, he is often referred to simply as the Prophet.

In addition to the revelations contained in the Qur'an, Muslims try to follow the example of Muhammad's life and sayings. These are known as the Sunna, from an Arabic word meaning "way" or "path." The Sunna are recounted in the Hadith, a collection of stories by Muhammad's companions or early Muslims, which describe how Muhammad lived and made decisions.

Muhammad was a strong and skillful military and political leader, but during his lifetime he generally attempted to resolve conflicts peacefully. Although he was involved in many military campaigns against the Meccans, Muhammad was often responding defensively to a treacherous and hostile environment. The Qur'an states clearly that peace is better than war; that war should be defensive, not offensive; and that treachery and betrayal are grave sins. The first 13 years of the Prophet's mission were nonviolent and peaceful—to the extent that the young Muslim community was nearly exterminated by intense persecution.

Muhammad's public conduct—his self-restraint and humility when in power, and his principled stands in the face of overwhelming odds—have established him in the imagination and historical consciousness of Muslims as a person to be revered. It is through his social relationships with the people around him that Muslims today get a sense of his character and personality. He was a husband, a friend, a father, and an adviser. He had friendships with men and women, he played with children, and he directed his community and close companions in what Muslims believe to be a life in the shadow of the Divine.

Within a century of his death, Islam had spread far beyond the Arabian Peninsula—the faith was practiced from Spain to China. If Muhammad had simply been a great military and political leader, the Arab Islamic empire would have faded as quickly as it had spread, much like the later Mongol Empire of the 13th century. Instead, Islam flourished not only as a religion but also as a civilization with rich traditions of scholarship, culture, and art. Today, followers of Islam make up the second-largest religious group in the world, with believers in nearly every country. It was the Prophet's upright character and his moral and ethical teachings that won—and continue to win—followers. The life of Muhammad changed the world forever.

 # Text-Dependent Questions

1. Who were the Quraysh? What importance did they have in Muhammad's life?
2. When and where did Muhammad receive his first revelations from Allah?
3. When did Muhammad begin to openly and publicly preach about his messages from Allah?
4. How did Muhammad live modestly? Provide some examples.

 # Research Project

Using your school library or the Internet, find out more about the Hashemites, as the descendants of the Prophet Muhammad are known. What is the origin of this clan, and how have they held political and economic power in the Arab world both in ancient times and in the present day?

3

Ali ibn Abi Talib

Although Muhammad never had a son, he did have a very close relationship with his younger cousin (and eventual son-in-law) Ali ibn Abi Talib. Ali's father, Abu Talib, had been Muhammad's uncle and had raised Muhammad after the death of the Prophet's grandfather.

Ali was born in Mecca in the year 600 to Abu Talib and his wife Fatima, who like Muhammad were members of the Hashimite clan. It is said that Fatima went into labor while on pilgrimage, and she gave birth to Ali in a secluded place in the Kaaba.

Muhammad had a great influence on Ali. According to some stories, the infant did not open his eyes until Muhammad held him, so Muhammad was the first person Ali ever saw. Muhammad is also said to have suggested the name Ali, a derivative of *Allah*, because the child had been born in the House of God.

Although little is known about Ali's early years, Muhammad was definitely involved in raising the youth. When Ali was five years old,

Opposite: Shiites perform the Friday noon prayers outside the shrine of Imam Ali in An Najaf, Iraq. The Shiites believe that Ali, Muhammad's son-in-law, was the first in a line of divinely appointed successors to the Prophet.

he joined Muhammad's family (this was a common custom of the time). When Ali was 10, he became the second person—and the first male—to accept Islam, after only Khadija. "The Prophet brought me up in his own arms and fed me with his own morsel," Ali later said. "I followed him, wherever he went, like a baby camel which follows its mother. Each day a new aspect of his character would beam out of his noble person and I would accept it and follow it as commanded."

Ali was not only one of the Prophet's earliest followers, but also one of the most committed. Even during the time of persecution at the hands of the Quraysh in Mecca, Ali remained faithful to Muhammad when others fell away. According to one story, when Muhammad left Mecca for Madina, he asked Ali to remain in Mecca. Twenty-two-year-old Ali agreed to sleep in Muhammad's bed, so that if the Quraysh came looking for the Prophet, they would believe he was still in Mecca. That night, while Ali slept soundly, Quraysh spies peeped through the windows and concluded that Muhammad was at home. They watched all night to make sure no one entered or left the house. The next morning, Quraysh soldiers surrounded Muhammad's house but were surprised when Ali, not Muhammad, emerged. The warriors, angry that they had been fooled by the ruse, wanted to kill Ali. But the Prophet's cousin faced the challenge with courage, and the Quraysh warriors soon withdrew.

Many other great acts of strength and courage are attributed to Ali. During the seventh century, battles were sometimes pre-

 Words to Understand in This Chapter

marriageable age—the age at which a person (especially a young woman) is allowed to marry, either by law or by custom. Among the Arab tribes at the time of Muhammad and Ali, girls as young as 12 years were permitted to marry.

plunder—money or valuables seized from conquered peoples or cities by a victorious army.

According to legend Ali was born within the ancient Kaaba, which is revered by Muslims as the House of God. The Kaaba is said to have originally been built by Adam, the first man, as a place of worship, and later rebuilt by Abraham and his son Ishmael after it was destroyed in the Great Flood.

ceded by individuals engaged in single combat. Muhammad often selected Ali as Islam's champion. Before the Battle of Badr, for example, Ali killed several Meccans in single combat; according to legend, in the full-scale battle that followed, Ali killed 21 men. In another example, a long siege against the Jewish stronghold at Khabir ended when Ali defeated the Jews' champion, Marhab, in single combat. It is written that Ali slew Marhab with one swing of his sword.

Ali also learned a great deal about military strategy from Muhammad, and he served as an important military aide during

A Persian miniature pictures Ali standing on the shoulders of the prophet Muhammad, in order to reach the idols in the Kaaba and throw them to the ground.

the wars against the Meccans. After Muhammad was wounded at the Battle of Uhud, Ali led a counterattack that prevented the Meccans from following up on their initial victory. Afterward, Muhammad praised him as *Asad Allah* (the Lion of God).

During this time, Muhammad's daughter Fatima reached ***marriageable age***. Several important followers of Muhammad requested permission to marry her, but Muhammad asked God for guidance. When Ali asked to take Fatima as his wife, Muhammad received a revelation that God approved of the marriage, and so the Prophet consented. Accounts of the time indicate that Ali had to sell his armor to raise the money needed for the marriage; Uthman, a wealthy Muslim trader, agreed to purchase the armor, then gave it back to Ali as a wedding gift. Ali and Fatima are said to have had a very happy marriage. Their first son, Hasan, was born in 625, and a second son, Hussain, was born the next year. The couple also had two daughters, as well as a son who died in infancy.

After Mecca surrendered to the Muslims in 630, Ali helped Muhammad remove the idols from the Kaaba. Some of the idols were too high for Muhammad to reach, so Ali stood on the Prophet's shoulders in order to smash them to the ground.

Selection of the Caliphs

When Muhammad died in 632, he had no sons; nor had he named a successor to guide the Muslims. Representatives of the Arab tribes gathered to name a leader, or caliph (from the Arabic *khalifa*, which means "successor"). Ali was a candidate. So was Abu Bakr, a longtime companion of the Prophet who was one of the first converts to Islam and a leader of the mosque in Madina, as well as Muhammad's father-in-law. A third candidate was Umar, a wealthy and influential citizen of Mecca and one of Muhammad's most trusted aides.

A group of Muslims supported Ali vigorously, believing that Muhammad had wished for Ali to be his successor. The issue threatened to divide the Arab tribes and destroy the new religion. To settle matters, Umar graciously withdrew his candidacy and said he would support Abu Bakr. Ali, disappointed, returned home to Madina.

During Abu Bakr's two-year reign as caliph, Ali was not much involved in political or military affairs. It is believed that he spent much of the time in religious devotion. He mourned the loss of Muhammad, who had been like a father, and he was devastated at the sudden death of his wife Fatima in 633. His relationship with Abu Bakr apparently warmed, however. After the caliph died in 634, Ali praised him in a funeral oration.

Umar ibn al-Khattab was chosen to succeed Abu Bakr as Islam's second caliph. During his reign Ali became more involved in politics. He served as chief justice and as Umar's closest adviser. He gave Umar a great deal of help in ruling the Muslims as they expanded their power east and west. In one instance, Umar considered removing some decorations from the Kaaba. He asked Ali for advice on the matter, and Ali said that when Muhammad had cleansed the Kaaba of idols, he had not touched the ornaments.

Because Muhammad had not objected to the decorations, Umar should not remove them from the House of God. Umar followed this advice. In recognition of all of Ali's good advice, Umar eventually wrote, "But for Ali, Umar would have been lost."

In 644 an assassin inflicted on Umar a wound that would eventually prove fatal. Before he died, however, Umar managed to call together the Prophet's six remaining close allies—including Ali—and entrusted them with the task of selecting the next caliph. Although Ali was again considered, Uthman, who had been married to two daughters of Muhammad and served as the Prophet's secretary, was ultimately chosen as the third caliph.

Uthman ruled for 11 years, presiding over a rebellious period in Islam. His reign ended in 656, when he was 84 years old. A large group of people who were unhappy with Uthman's administration made their way to Mecca, where they demanded that the caliph abdicate, or step down. When Uthman refused, he was murdered in his home.

With the leadership position vacant, Ali was offered the caliphate. He declined, so it was offered to several other candidates. All of them likewise refused. Ali eventually agreed to become the fourth caliph after delegations of Muslims from Madina and other provinces urged him to accept.

Ali was 56 years old when he became caliph. For most of the past quarter-century he had lived in peace at his home in Madina. Now he would be faced with the difficult job of putting down many rebellions.

Reign of the Fourth Caliph

During his nearly five years as caliph, Ali did much to expand Muslim culture and science. He wrote poetry and taught his followers how to recite and better understand the Qur'an. He was devoted to the education of his people and used the resources of his government to pay for the schooling of some 2,000 students in Kufa, a city in present-day Iraq. (He had moved the government from Madina to Kufa because many of his supporters lived there.)

Ali was an influential jurist. He established a code of Islamic laws, and he founded a system of courts throughout the Arabian Peninsula. Ali also built forts, cut roads through wilderness areas, and oversaw construction of a bridge over the Euphrates River. He harbored an interest in astronomy, espousing the theory that life

Ali became Islam's fourth caliph after the murder of Uthman, who is pictured here holding a copy of the Qur'an. Like that of his predecessor, Ali's reign was filled with strife.

This manuscript illustration shows Ali and his supporters fighting against their adversaries. Ali spent much of his time as caliph trying to keep the Muslims united under his rule.

exists on other stars and that each star in the sky is separated by a distance that would take 250 years to cover.

Unfortunately, Ali spent much of his time as caliph fighting wars and putting down rebellions. The first great test of Ali's authority came late in the year 656 near Basra, in present-day Iraq. Ayesha, a wife of the prophet Muhammad who held a long-standing antagonism toward Ali, waged the challenge. She was joined by two of Ali's rivals, the tribal leaders Zubayr and Talha. Each man desired to obtain the rank of caliph for himself.

A clash between Ali's supporters and Ayesha's army erupted in the early-morning hours of December 4. At first, Ali commanded his men to fight only in self-defense. He also told his soldiers to spare the wounded and ordered them to seize no *plunder* from the enemy. Even as a shower of arrows started falling on his men, Ali told them to stand fast.

The leaders of the rebellion believed their men would fight hardest if they could see the widow of the Prophet leading the attack, so Ayesha took a personal role in the battle. Sitting atop a camel, Ayesha rode throughout the battlefield, exhorting the rebels to throw themselves at Ali's soldiers. At first, the tactic was successful. It seemed that wherever Ayesha's camel appeared on the battlefield, the fighting was at its fiercest.

Ali realized that Ayesha had to be removed from the battlefield, so he dispatched a single warrior with explicit orders: do not kill Ayesha, but bring down the camel. The warrior accomplished this by cutting off the camel's legs. With Ayesha no longer in view atop the camel, the rebellious soldiers soon lost heart and the battle ended. Zubayr and Talha were killed in the fighting. Rather than put Ayesha to death after the battle, however, Ali chose to show mercy. He sent Ayesha back to her home in Madina, where she lived the rest of her life quietly in devotion to Islam.

The Battle of the Camel was an important victory for Ali, but challenges to his rule would continue. One of his first acts as caliph had been to dismiss provincial governors, many of whom were members of the Umayyad clan, longtime rivals of the Hashimites.

One of the complaints against Uthman was that he had appointed too many Umayyads to high-ranking positions. Ali did not trust the Umayyads, particularly Muawiya, governor of Syria.

When Muawiya learned that he had lost his position, he refused to step down. Instead, he encouraged the Syrians to rise up against Ali. Muawiya charged that the fourth caliph had failed to avenge the death of Uthman. In a mosque in Damascus, Muawiya delivered a feverish sermon designed to incite hatred against Ali. During the sermon, Muawiya displayed the bloodstained shirt Uthman had been wearing at the time of his murder. He also displayed the severed fingers of Uthman's wife Nalia, which she had lost while trying to defend her husband.

Some 120,000 Syrians joined Muawiya's army. He led them to the valley of Siffin along the western bank of the Euphrates River. Ali's army numbered 80,000 men, most of them recruited from Kufa.

The two armies remained in a stalemate for 110 days. During that period, Ali attempted many times to negotiate a settlement with Muawiya. He offered to turn their differences over to Islamic scholars, who would resolve the dispute by consulting the Qur'an. Muawiya refused. While the generals talked, the two sides skirmished nearly every day, costing each army thousands of lives. Ali offered to end the bloodshed through single combat. Again, Muawiya refused. Finally, after protracted negotiations, Ali concluded that he could not come to terms with Muawiya. On July 26, 657, the two sides clashed in the Battle of Siffin.

As a youth, Ali had been a fierce warrior in the service of the Prophet. Even though he was now 57 years old, he fought with great strength and exhorted his men to fight bravely. Ali rode a white-headed horse into battle. Whenever he killed an enemy soldier, he would shout, "God is victorious." Witnesses on the battlefield later swore that they heard him shout those words 400 times.

Although Ali's soldiers were outnumbered, by the third day Muawiya realized his men were losing the battle. He resorted to a tactic he knew would stop Ali's soldiers and save his Syrian army from destruction: he ordered men in the front lines to push pages of the Qur'an onto the tips of their lances. Ali saw through the ruse immediately and admonished his men to keep fighting. But the Muslims refused to raise their swords against the Qur'an, and the Battle of Siffin ended in a stalemate. Both sides sent representatives to a meeting to negotiate a peace treaty.

Ali led his men back to Kufa, but on the march home he was faced with rebellion in the ranks of his followers. A group of disgruntled men were angry that Muawiya had not been defeated and that Ali had agreed to arbitration of his claim to the caliphate. They also complained that Muslim leaders had kept the plunder from conquered cities, rather than distributing it to the soldiers. Ali tried to settle their complaints, but he soon found that these dissenters could not be satisfied. About 12,000 men left Ali's camp; they became known as Kharijites (from an Arabic word meaning "seceders.")

A few months later, the arbitrators met to settle the dispute between Ali and Muawiya. Ali's representative was outmaneuvered by Muawiya's delegate, who announced that an election for a new caliph would be held. When the decision was announced, Muawiya's followers declared him caliph. Once again, Ali raised an army to fight Muawiya and his supporters.

First, however, Ali decided to deal with the Kharijites. His army caught up with them near Naharwan, a small town east of the Tigris River. At the Battle of Naharwan in 658, Ali's men slaughtered many of the Kharijites, although some did manage to escape.

While the caliph pursued the Kharijites, Muawiya launched an offensive into Egypt, dispatching 6,000 warriors to depose Ali's appointed governor, Muhammad ibn Abu Bakr, the son of the first caliph. Ali sent his own men to help the governor fend off the attack, but they arrived too late. Muawiya's men murdered Muhammad ibn Abu Bakr, and Muawiya now controlled the resources of both Egypt and Syria.

Basra soon fell to Muawiya as well. When Basra's governor,

Ziyad ibn Abihi, sent 2,000 men to Kufa to help guard Ali, Muawiya took advantage and dispatched a contingent to Ziyad's city. His men arrived to find Basra unguarded; they simply took over.

Now Muawiya believed himself strong enough to attack Ali in Kufa. Soldiers from the two sides skirmished many times in the countryside surrounding the city. Ali often personally led parties of soldiers into the territory near the city to help fend off the attacks. Meanwhile, Muawiya extended his control in the Arabian Peninsula. His men captured Madina and Mecca, as well as cities as far south as Yemen. By 660 Muawiya had declared himself caliph.

Ali's Death and the Schism in Islam

Ali made plans to attack his longtime enemy in Syria, but he would never get the chance. Kharijite survivors who had taken refuge in Mecca were making their own plans for revenge. They decided to assassinate Ali, Muawiya, and Amr ibn al-'As, the military leader who conquered Egypt and later became Muawiya's adviser and arbitrator in the negotiations with Ali. A Kharijite assassin found Muawiya in a Damascus mosque; the ruler was wounded but survived the attack. Amr ibn al-'As also survived an attack—his would-be assassin did not know his target and killed another man by mistake.

In Kufa, however, a Kharijite assassin found Ali praying alone in a mosque just before dawn. The killer waited until Ali was prostrate in prayer, then struck him with a poisoned sword. When the other members of the mosque arrived for prayer, they found the body of the slain caliph.

Tradition holds that before his death Ali, sensing the end was near, told his followers to place his body on the back of a camel and allow the camel to roam free. Ali's wish was granted, and the camel bearing his body finally stopped in An Najaf, a city about 100 miles south of Baghdad. Today, the caliph's tomb is located within a magnificent gold-domed shrine, a place of deep reverence to the followers of Ali.

Muawiya recovered from his wounds and assumed the caliphate. After ascending to the leadership position, he founded a ruling dynasty (the Umayyads) that would last for generations; it finally lost power around 750. A descendant of Muawiya would establish a Muslim kingdom on the Iberian Peninsula (present-day

Afghanistan's Shiites claim that this 15th-century mosque at Mazar-e-Sharif contains the tomb of Ali. Others believe that Ali's final resting place is in An Najaf, Iraq. In any case, Shiites—who make up about 14 percent of Muslims worldwide—are unified in their conviction that religious authority rightfully passed through Ali and his descendants.

Spain) that would be the greatest and most enlightened civilization of Europe at the time.

The death of Ali would lead to an important schism in Islam. Ali had always had a large group of supporters, who became known as *Shiat Ali* (the party of Ali). After his death many of Ali's followers refused to accept the legitimacy of Muawiya as Islam's leader, instead supporting the claim of Ali's son Hasan to the caliphate. But under the threat of the Umayyads' military power, Hasan renounced his claim to the caliphate and retired to Madina, where he died around 669. At that time Ali's followers declared his other son, Hussain, the rightful caliph. However, Muawiya announced that his son Yazid would be the next successor, and after Muawiya's death in 680, followers of Yazid and supporters of Hussain met at the Battle of Karbala, in present-day Iraq. Yazid's forces slaughtered their outnumbered rivals, and Hussain himself was killed.

But a minority of Muslims continued to believe that Islam's rightful leaders should come only from the family of the Prophet, through the line of Ali and Muhammad's daughter Fatima. Eventually this group, known as the Shiites, would develop a religious doctrine based on the authority and sinlessness of Ali and his descendants (referred to as imams). Over the centuries the Shiites and Islam's largest sect, the Sunnis, developed distinct theological schools, and their relations would at times be strained and even hostile.

Today about 14 percent of the world's Muslims are Shiites. Most live in Iraq, Iran, India, Lebanon, and Bahrain, although there are significant communities in other Muslim countries.

The Significance of Ali

Ali is among Islam's most significant figures and is revered by Sunnis and Shiites alike. His bravery and skill in battle helped prevent the early Muslim community from being overwhelmed by its enemies; his piety is unquestioned. As one of Muhammad's closest living relatives, and one of the Prophet's earliest converts, Ali believed that he understood exactly what God had envisioned for Islam and for the Muslim community. His death marked the end of a golden age in Islam—the time of *al-khulafa' al-rashidun* (the rightly guided caliphs). These first four caliphs had all known Muhammad personally and had worked with him to establish the Islamic community. Their combined rule, from 632 to 661, was marked by great cultural accomplishments and by the remarkable spread of Islam.

But Ali is especially revered by Shiites, who consider him the first Imam as well as a martyr to their faith.

Text-Dependent Questions

1. How many enemy soldiers is Ali believed to have killed during the Battle of Badr?
2. After Muhammad's death in 632, what Muslim leader succeeded him as the first caliph?
3. To what city did Ali move the Muslim government after becoming caliph in 656?

Research Project

In Islam, a caliphate is a theocratic state in which the ruler (known as a caliph), has authority over both the spiritual and temporal lives of his subjects and all people must obey Islamic laws. The organization ISIL has declared that it is forming a new caliphate, to which all Muslims must pledge allegiance. Find a world map online, and identify the ten countries with the greatest population of Muslims (Indonesia, Pakistan, India, Bangladesh, Egypt, Nigeria, Iran, Turkey, Algeria, and Morocco. How close are these countries to the lands where ISIL holds territory, Iraq and Syria?

4

Rabia al-Adawiyya

It is said that one night, while Rabia al-Adawiyya slept, a thief broke into her home and picked up her veil. As he turned to leave, the thief discovered he could not find the door because a darkness had fallen all around him. When the thief put down the veil, the room brightened and he could see the door. He picked up the veil again to make his getaway, but again the room darkened. Seven times he put down the veil, then retrieved it, but each time he held the veil the path to his escape became clouded. Finally, from a corner of the room, an unseen voice said, "O man, do not trouble thyself since for all these years she has entrusted herself to Us and Satan has not had the courage to go round about her and shall a thief have the courage to go round about her veil? Concern not thyself with her, O pick-pocket, if one friend is asleep another friend is awake and keeping watch."

The story of the thief and the veil is one of many miracles said to have occurred in the presence of Rabia al-Adawiyya, an eighth-cen-

Opposite: Indian Muslims worship at the shrine of a Sufi saint. The eighth-century Sufi master Rabia al-Adawiyya was one of the first, and most influential, Sufis.

tury woman whose devotion to Allah was so complete that she has achieved the status of sainthood in the eyes of Muslims. Rabia was one of the first Sufis—Muslims who believe the path to God can be found by surrendering their lives completely to prayer and exaltation of Allah.

Hard Times

Islamic tradition holds that the first miracle associated with Rabia occurred soon after her birth, in the year 717. She was born into a poor family in the city of Basra, in present-day Iraq. Her parents named her Rabia, an Arabic word meaning "fourth," because she was their fourth daughter. The family was so poor that they had no oil to light the lamp in the house, nor did they own swaddling clothes with which to wrap the newborn child. Her mother sent Rabia's father, Ismail, to a neighbor's house to ask for lamp oil, but her father believed, in the Sufi tradition, that God would supply all the family's needs. When he returned home, he told his wife that the neighbor had refused to answer the door.

That night, as Ismail slept, he had a vision in which the prophet Muhammad told him, "Don't be sorrowful, for this daughter who is born is a great saint, whose intercession will be desired by 70,000 of my community." The Prophet then instructed Ismail to write to Isa Zadhan, the *emir* of Basra, and tell him that as punishment for neglecting his prayers he was to give money to Ismail. After Rabia's father awoke, he wrote the letter as the Prophet had directed. When the emir read the letter, he

 Words to Understand in This Chapter

emir—a prince; a Muslim ruler, chief, or commander.

mysticism—the belief that direct knowledge of God can be attained through subjective experience; the experience of direct communion with the Supreme Being.

realized the error of his ways and personally delivered the money to Ismail's humble home.

Despite their sudden good fortune, Rabia's family soon faced hard times. While Rabia was still a child, her parents died and a famine swept through Basra. Rabia turned to begging on the streets, where she was kidnapped and sold into slavery.

Her master made her work very hard. Throughout her ordeal, Rabia's devotion to God remained strong. She refused to eat during the day and spent her evenings deep in prayer. One night, her master awoke and, looking through the window of his house, saw Rabia standing in worship. He heard her say, "O my Lord, Thou knowest that the desire of my heart is to obey Thee, and that the light of my eye is in the service of Thy court. If the matter rested with me, I should not cease for one hour from Thy service, but Thou hast made me subject to a creature."

Rabia's master then saw a lamp dangling over the girl's head, illuminating his house. He saw there were no strings holding the lamp. The next morning, Rabia's master freed her from slavery.

A Life of Devotion

After making a pilgrimage to Mecca, Rabia returned to Basra, where she dedicated herself completely to finding the true path to God. She lived a simple life of poverty, refusing even her friends' offerings of food, clothing, and other necessities because she believed that God would provide for her. She refused to marry, stating that a husband and family would detract from her devotion to God. Rabia embraced the mystical way of Sufism, and she taught others how to travel this path to union with God.

Rabia's singular devotion to God is illustrated by the many stories of miracles that occurred throughout her life (though it should be emphasized that Muslims do not believe Rabia herself performed any miracles, as that is something only God can do). One story recounts how, while on her way to Mecca during the *hajj*, Rabia was stranded in the desert when her donkey died. Many

The Sufi Tradition

Sufism, an Islamic mystical tradition emphasizing inner spirituality as a path to God, arose partly as a reaction to the excesses of the leaders who came after Ali, the fourth and last of the rightly guided caliphs. The early Sufis were troubled by the habits of the Umayyad caliphs and other religious leaders who seemed to prefer lives of luxury to simple devotion to God. What's more, the Sufis questioned whether any intermediary should serve between them and Allah; even the rituals of the mosque represented an obstacle that separated them from God. The Sufis had no desire for wealth or power; the only reward they sought was the union of their soul with God.

Over the centuries, some Sufis surrendered their lives completely to God, spending all of their time in prayer and devotion. For example, the Sufi master Abu Said ibn Abi al-Khayr (967–1049) discovered Sufism at the age of 26 when he heard an Islamic scholar recite this verse from the Qur'an: "Say Allah! Then leave them to amuse themselves in their vain discourse."

Abu Said had been a scholar himself, reading extensively and collecting hundreds of books. When he turned to mysticism, Abu Said collected his books and burned them. "The first step in Sufism is the breaking of inkpots, the tearing up of books, the forgetting of all kinds of knowledge," he said. He then spent much of the next 14 years of his life devoting himself completely to the worship of God. For the first seven years, he claimed to have sat alone in his room, constantly chanting "Allah . . . Allah . . . Allah" over and over again. He never changed his clothes, never spoke to others unless absolutely necessary, and ate only after nightfall—and then only a small piece of bread. Sometimes at night he would lower himself into a well and recite the entire Qur'an. At the age of 40 he decided to preach to others and founded a monastery devoted to Sufi worship.

Sufism has endured over the centuries. Today, many Muslims adhere to Sufi principles. Though most have adapted their lifestyles to conform to 21st-century society, the spirit of Sufi worship has not changed. For most Sufis, prayer is a personal, soul-cleansing rite practiced in extreme devotion to Allah.

Turkish Sufis perform a whirling dance called the Sema. Sufis believe that through dancing, chanting, meditation, and other practices they can achieve union with Allah.

travelers passed, all offering to take her with them. In each case, however, Rabia refused, insisting that she needed to rely only on Allah for deliverance. She prayed to God, asking Him for help. As soon as she completed her prayer, the donkey returned to life and Rabia was able to continue her journey to Mecca.

Many stories concern Rabia's ability to illuminate a room without the use of lamps. On one occasion, the glow from her fingertips is said to have provided light for a room. On another occasion, witnesses reported that Rabia was able to cook a meal without lighting a fire.

Rabia always denied that she possessed extraordinary powers. Zulfa bint Abd al-Wahid, her niece, recounted the following conversation with Rabia on the matter:

> I said to Rabia, "O my aunt, why do you not allow people to visit you?" Rabia replied, "I fear lest when I am dead, people will relate of me what I did not say or do, what if I had seen, I should have feared or mistrusted. I am told that they say that I find money under my place of prayer, and that I cook in the pot without a fire." I said to her, "They relate of you that you find food and drink in your house," and she said, "O, daughter of my brother, if I had found such things in my house I would not have touched them, or laid hands upon them, but I tell you that I buy things and am blessed in them."

Many stories are told about Rabia and other Sufis. One story involves Ibrahim ibn al-Adham, who took 40 years to make his pilgrimage to Mecca. Ibrahim continually delayed himself because he stopped so often to pray along the way. When he arrived in Mecca, he discovered that the Kaaba was missing. At first Ibrahim suspected that some calamity had occurred and that the Kaaba had been destroyed. An unseen voice assured him that this was not the case. "No harm has befallen your eyes," said the voice, "but the Kaaba has gone to meet a woman, who is approaching this place."

When the woman arrived, Ibrahim saw that it was Rabia and that the Kaaba had returned to its rightful place. Ibrahim accused Rabia of causing a disturbance in the world that had resulted in the removal of the Kaaba, but Rabia told Ibrahim that it was his act of delaying his hajj that had caused the disturbance. When Ibrahim answered that his constant prayer had caused the delay, Rabia responded that his prayers had been merely rituals, and that she had been able to cross the desert quickly because of her devotion to God.

An aging Sufi master known as Hasan of Basra plays a role in

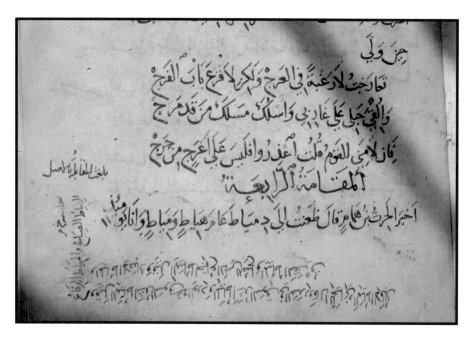

Many Muslims still read and enjoy the poetry of Rabia al-Adawiyya.

many of the stories told about Rabia. Hasan was much older than Rabia—he died when she was just 11 years old—but many of the stories show that she was the wiser of the two Sufis.

In most of the stories in which Hasan appears, he commits some error while devoting himself to God and is corrected by Rabia. For example, at one meeting Hasan shows Rabia that he can sit atop his prayer mat while it floats on water. Rabia responds by showing Hasan she can sit atop her prayer mat while it floats on air. Then she scolds him, telling him that the truly devoted should concern themselves with matters of far more importance.

Hasan greatly admired Rabia for the purity of her soul. "I passed one whole night and day with Rabia speaking of the 'Way and the Truth,' and it never passed through my mind that I was a man nor did it occur to me that she was a woman, and at the end when I looked at her, I saw myself [spiritually] bankrupt, and Rabia as truly sincere," he said.

Although Hasan died while Rabia was still a young girl, he sometimes appears in stories about the later years of her life. One story even suggests that Hasan visited Rabia's bedside shortly before her death.

Rabia is believed to have died in the year 801, at the age of 84. She had been ill for some time, and friends were keeping vigil around her bed. Just before she died, however, she asked them all to leave the room. When they closed the door behind them, her friends heard her say, "O soul at rest, return to thy Lord, satisfied with Him, giving satisfaction to Him. So enter among My servants and enter into My Paradise."

From Fear to Love

Rabia al-Adawiyya had a significant and lasting impact on the development of Islam—in particular, on the religion's mystical tradition. Previously, Islamic mystics had been driven by fear of God. Rabia stressed love of God, transforming the focus of Islamic *mysticism* and providing a powerful example for those who came after her to emulate.

 ## Text-Dependent Questions

1. Where and when was Rabia al-Adawiyya born?
2. What is Sufism? What does it emphasize?
3. Who was Hasan of Basra?

 ## Research Project

Using the Internet or your school library, do some research on the Islamic mysticism known as Sufism. What do Sufis believe, and how does this differ from the beliefs of other Muslims? Write a two-page report and present it to your class.

5

Salah al-Din

I n the five centuries after the death of Muhammad, Islam had spread far beyond the Arabian Peninsula and into Africa, Asia, and Europe. But the unity of the original Arab Muslim empire had disintegrated. For example, many Sunni Muslims in Syria and the Arabian Peninsula recognized the authority of the Abbasid caliphs in Baghdad. In Egypt, however, the Fatimid dynasty had come to power in 909; these rulers followed the Ismaili sect of Shiite Islam. Other Muslim sects or groups, both Shiite and Sunni, followed different leaders.

In addition to disagreements and rivalries from within, the Islamic world was under pressure from without. In the year 1095, knights from Europe launched the First Crusade, an invasion of Muslim-controlled lands in the name of Christianity. By 1099 the Crusaders had taken control over Jerusalem and other important cities and principalities along the eastern Mediterranean coast. For the next five decades, Christian Crusader kingdoms separated Muslims in Egypt

Opposite: The walls of Saone, a Crusader castle in present-day Syria. In 1188 this castle was captured by a Muslim army commanded by the great Kurdish general Salah al-Din.

and Africa from Muslims in Syria, Arabia, and the East.

In 1138, in the midst of this tumultuous era, a boy named Salah al-Din Yusuf ibn Ayyub—better known today as Salah al-Din (or, in the West, Saladin)—was born. By the time he died 55 years later, Salah al-Din would rule a vast Islamic empire, uniting Muslims with a fierce resolve while using his intelligence and guile to turn them against a common enemy.

Salah al-Din was not an Arab but a Kurd. (The Kurds, who are predominantly Sunni Muslims, have traditionally survived as nomadic herders in the rugged, mountainous region known as Kurdistan, which includes significant parts of the modern-day states of Turkey, Iran, and Iraq, as well as small sections of Syria and Armenia.)

Salah al-Din's father, Najim al-Din Ayyub, and his father's brother Shirkuh were men of rank in the government established by Zinki, a former Kurdish slave who had risen to power in Syria. The two men earned Zinki's favor when they rescued him from assassins. The ruler rewarded Najim al-Din by appointing him commander of the city of Baalbek in present-day Lebanon, while Shirkuh became an aide to Zinki's son, Nur al-Din. When Zinki was murdered and Nur al-Din became ruler of Syria, Najim al-Din was appointed governor of Damascus, where Salah al-Din grew up. While still a teenager, Salah al-Din served as a military aide to his uncle.

Intrigues

In 1160 an 11-year-old boy named al-Adid became the Fatimid caliph of Cairo. Al-Adid sought to appoint a *vizier* to run his gov-

Words to Understand in This Chapter

minaret—a tall tower in a mosque.

vizier—a high official serving a Muslim ruler.

Godfrey of Bouillon (center, on horseback), the leader of the Crusaders, gives thanks to God after breaching the defenses of Jerusalem in July 1099. When the Crusaders captured the city, they slaughtered the Muslims and Jews within.

ernment. The holder of this post would have great power in Egypt. Two men emerged as the top candidates: Dirgam and Shawar. Dirgam, a master of palace intrigues, prevailed over his rival, forcing Shawar to flee to Damascus, where he sought to ally himself with Nur al-Din. In Cairo, Dirgam purged the Egyptian army of officers whose loyalty he suspected. This would prove to be a serious error, because in the years to come Egypt's army would lack leadership and prove incapable of defending the kingdom.

To the north, the Christians of the Latin Kingdom of Jerusalem, under King Amalric, had emerged as a threat to Fatimid rule. In Damascus, Shawar convinced Nur al-Din to help him oust Dirgam, arguing that a Syrian invasion of Egypt would help bolster the country against the Christians. Nur al-Din assigned the job to Salah al-Din's uncle Shirkuh, who led an invasion of Egypt in April 1164. He was accompanied by Salah al-Din, now 26 years old and his uncle's most trusted military aide.

The Fatimids were no match for Shirkuh's Syrian horsemen; resistance was quickly swept aside. So was Dirgam. Shawar became the new vizier, and he immediately started making plans to get rid of Shirkuh and Salah al-Din.

The wily vizier found an ally in Amalric; he convinced the Christian king to attack Shirkuh. The two armies fought a battle at Bilbais in Egypt. Shirkuh's Syrians would never have been able to stand up against Amalric's superior force, but Salah al-Din's uncle was saved at the last minute by Nur al-Din, who launched an attack on Jerusalem. Amalric was forced to withdraw from the battle so that his army could hurry home and defend his kingdom.

When Shirkuh and Salah al-Din returned to Damascus, they convinced the Sunni caliph to declare war against the Egyptians. In January 1167, Shirkuh led 2,000 Syrian warriors against a combined Fatimid-Christian army at Ashmunein in Egypt. During the battle, he relied heavily on his nephew, who showed both courage and tactical skill in the field.

Amalric soon signed a treaty with Nur al-Din, ensuring that his kingdom would not be attacked from the north. The Christian king then turned his attention to the south and began a brutal attack on Egypt. The vizier Shawar once again asked Nur al-Din for help. Although the Syrians had declared war against the Fatimids, Nur al-Din agreed to protect Egypt—for a price. Shawar was forced to promise the Syrian leader a third of his country's wealth in exchange for saving Egypt from the Christian invaders. Again, Nur al-Din handed the job to Shirkuh, who swept into Egypt at the head of an 8,000-man Syrian army. Salah al-Din rode at his uncle's side.

Realizing he was outnumbered, Amalric retreated to Jerusalem. His abortive invasion proved politically costly. For the first time, the two warring Muslim factions had united against a common Christian enemy.

Yet within the Islamic world, envy and suspicion also reigned. In Egypt, Shirkuh and Shawar soon started plotting against each other. Shirkuh struck first: in early 1169, his nephew Salah al-Din kidnapped the vizier, took him to a tent in the desert, and had him beheaded. The position of vizier now went to Shirkuh.

Back in Damascus, Nur al-Din was furious. The Syrian ruler had sought to spread Sunni Islam into Egypt, but the Shiite Fatimid ruler still enjoyed sovereignty, with Shirkuh as his vizier. What's more, it was clear that Shirkuh had used the Syrian army to attain power for himself. However, Shirkuh would not live long

As vizier of Egypt, Salah al-Din had to put down several challenges to his authority. He proved to be a shrewd and strong leader.

enough to enjoy his newfound position. He died on March 23, 1169, about three months after becoming vizier.

Salah al-Din's Rise to Power

Al-Adid's Shiite advisers urged the Fatimid caliph to appoint Salah al-Din as the new vizier, believing that of all the candidates the young Kurd could most easily be controlled. That turned out to be a woeful miscalculation of Salah al-Din's character.

Salah al-Din's first move as vizier was to raise his own army, composed of men whose loyalty to him would be assured. He was

The walls of the Citadel of Cairo were built at Salah al-Din's direction. As Egypt's military grew stronger under Salah al-Din, fighting among the Muslims seemed inevitable. However, the death of Nur al-Din gave Salah al-Din an opportunity to unite them under his control.

able to accomplish this task by throwing open Egypt's treasury. At the time, the Egyptian army was composed of 40,000 Fatimid cavalry soldiers and 30,000 Sudanese infantrymen. The head of the infantry, Mu'tamin al-Khilafa, saw his chance now to lead an uprising against Salah al-Din, believing the young vizier too weak to put down a rebellion. For the Sudanese commander, it would be a fatal mistake. Salah al-Din suppressed the revolt, had Mu'tamin arrested and executed, and scattered his troops.

The next move was made by Nur al-Din. He ordered Salah al-Din to decree the Sunni caliph of Baghdad the spiritual leader of Egypt. If the Shiite ruler al-Adid had a complaint about this sudden challenge to his authority, it would soon be of little consequence. In September 1171, just as the first Sunni prayers were to be said in Cairo's mosques, al-Adid contracted a mysterious illness and died. The caliph was just 22 years old.

With al-Adid out of the way, Salah al-Din was now the unquestioned leader of Egypt. Still, he lacked the military strength to conquer lands beyond Egypt's borders, and the armies of Nur al-Din were a serious threat. Between 1171 and 1174 Egypt and Syria moved close to war. Twice during that time, Nur al-Din called on Salah al-Din to join him in attacks on Christian-held cities; both times Salah al-Din refused, knowing perhaps that by putting his men in close proximity to Nur al-Din's troops he would expose them to danger. His refusal to follow Nur al-Din's orders infuriated the Syrian leader.

Finally, Nur al-Din sent emissaries to Cairo demanding a high tribute from Egypt's treasury. War between the two Muslim realms now appeared inevitable. The threat to Salah al-Din's rule was averted by a fortunate turn of events: the death of Nur al-Din.

Nur al-Din's rightful heir was Al-Malik al-Salih, his 11-year-old son, but in Damascus a battle for power soon developed among Nur al-Din's nephews and some of the army's highest-ranking leaders. The Christians of Jerusalem might have invaded at this time, but when Amalric died suddenly a few months after

Nur al-Din, the Crusaders were in no position to launch an attack. For Salah al-Din, the opportunity to take Syria was at hand. In October 1174 he rode into Damascus at the head of a column of 700 cavalry soldiers. He took the city with no bloodshed, accomplishing this feat by purchasing the loyalty of Damascus's Syrian defenders, who directed their men to now fight under Salah al-Din.

Salah al-Din had taken Damascus, but there were many other cities where Muslim princes were not so willing to pledge fealty to the Kurd. They vowed to fight, and for the next 12 years much blood would be spilled. In nearly every case, however, Salah al-Din prevailed. He scored his first great victory in April 1175, when his men clashed with an army from the city of Mosul in Iraq. Salah al-Din proved himself an excellent field general, and he was able to inspire among his men great confidence in his leadership. Other battlefield victories soon followed.

But Salah al-Din's talents were not confined to the battlefield. He also showed great skill in the more subtle art of diplomacy, and his pragmatic approach often enabled him to attain his objectives with a minimum of bloodshed. An illustrative example is his taking of the Syrian city of Aleppo in 1183.

In 1181 Nur al-Din's 19-year-old son al-Salih died. He had hated Salah al-Din since the death of his own father, and on his deathbed al-Salih urged his followers to resist Salah al-Din. The center for that resistance would be Aleppo, a heavily fortified city under the command of al-Salih's designated successor, Izz al-Din.

As he approached Aleppo at the head of a 5,000-man army, Salah al-Din understood that the city's defenses would be overcome only after an enormous loss of life on both sides. After an initial assault, he suddenly called off the attack and sought an end to the conflict through negotiation. Salah al-Din found that Izz al-Din had little desire to fight. Moreover, the people of Aleppo had no love for their ruler and wished him to be gone. So Salah al-Din permitted Izz al-Din to plunder the city's treasury and march away peacefully with his followers. On June 11, 1183, Salah al-Din and his army entered Aleppo through the city's gates.

By 1187 Salah al-Din had succeeded in uniting Egypt and Syria under his control. His status as a brave warrior and military genius was almost universally acknowledged, but he was also regarded as a just and wise ruler. His subjects found him to be an honest man who always kept his word. He also lived simply and kept no treasures for himself, evidently heeding lessons he had learned as he saw the wealthy but corrupt Fatimid reign in Egypt crumble. Salah al-Din was also a devout Muslim, remembered for his consciousness of Allah and his personal sense of piety.

Fighting the Crusaders

After the death of Amalric, the Latin Kingdom of Jerusalem became embroiled in its own internal squabbles. In 1186 the

This illustration from a 14th-century French manuscript shows cavalry soldiers from the army of Salah al-Din. With the Muslims of Egypt and Syria united, in 1187 Salah al-Din turned his attention to the Crusader kingdoms that had been established along the eastern Mediterranean nearly 100 years earlier.

knight Guy de Lusignan took the throne of Jerusalem. The leader of another Crusader kingdom would set in motion the events that would culminate in war between Christians and Muslims, however. Reginald of Chatillon ruled over the city of Karak, just east of the Dead Sea in what is now Jordan. In 1183 he infuriated Muslims when he sent knights into Madina to destroy the prophet Muhammad's tomb. At Madina, Reginald's men were met and slaughtered by an Egyptian army. In 1186 Reginald again antagonized Muslims when he attacked a caravan, stole its cargo, and took several Muslim prisoners. Among the captives were Salah al-Din's sister. Salah al-Din swore to kill Reginald.

The armies of Reginald and Guy de Lusignan met Salah al-Din's army at Hattin, just east of Nazareth in what is now Israel, on July 4, 1187. Again, Salah al-Din displayed a genius on the battlefield that the Christian commanders could not

A tomb carving of King Richard I of England, leader of the Third Crusade and Salah al-Din's most famous opponent. The Third Crusade ended in a stalemate, with the Europeans unable to recapture Jerusalem from Salah al-Din's forces.

match. The Muslim leader cut off the Christians from water supplies, started fires to blind them with black smoke, and wore them down during the intense midsummer heat. Reginald and Guy were captured during the battle and brought before Salah al-Din. To Guy he offered a drink of water, the promise of a pardon, and a pledge to work out a truce. Reginald of Chatillon, however, was beheaded.

Salah al-Din had always been vocal about his desire to repel the European Crusaders from their kingdoms along the Mediterranean coast and to liberate Jerusalem. However, he was not interested in waging war against Christian Arabs, or even against Western Christians who did not invade Muslim lands or occupy Jerusalem. Many Christian Arab villages existed around the Crusader kingdoms, and Salah al-Din allied himself with the people of these villages. In addition, several of Salah al-Din's top generals were Christian Arabs.

Following his victory at Hattin, Salah al-Din's forces struck the coastal Christian city of Acre. Then he moved on to Jerusalem. The battle lasted just 12 days before the Christians surrendered. Salah al-Din proved far more merciful than the Crusaders had been when they took Jerusalem in 1099 and went on a killing rampage, massacring virtually all of the city's Muslim and Jewish inhabitants. Salah al-Din seized the city's gold as ransom for prisoners captured during the siege, but he ultimately released most of the prisoners whose ransoms could not be paid. Guy de Lusignan pledged an oath not to bear arms against Salah al-Din. Jews were permitted to return to Jerusalem.

In response to the loss of Jerusalem, European rulers launched the Third Crusade. In 1191 the army of King Richard I of England besieged Acre, eventually forcing the city's Muslim defenders to surrender. Richard's forces proceeded to defeat Muslims at the coastal city of Jaffa and near Arsuf. The British king next turned his attention to the ultimate prize: Jerusalem. By January 1192 Richard had advanced to within 12 miles of the Holy City, but bad weather, the threat of an attack from Salah al-Din, and an army of

Muslim reinforcements compelled him to pull back. In June, Richard mounted another push to take Jerusalem, but it became clear that his army wasn't large enough to besiege the city. For his part, Salah al-Din—recognizing that time was on his side—avoided engaging Richard in a major battle near Jerusalem. By early July, Richard had decided to withdraw and seek a treaty with Salah al-Din.

Several battles would be fought before a final agreement was hammered out, including one at Jaffa, where Richard's badly outnumbered forces staved off repeated Muslim attempts to overrun the city. It was at Jaffa and in the aftermath of the fighting that Salah al-Din cemented his reputation among Europeans for chivalry and generosity toward his foes. When Richard emerged from his lines with only a handful of mounted knights to lead a counterattack, Salah al-Din was so moved by the English king's bravery that, seeing Richard's horse killed beneath him, Salah al-Din immediately had two additional mounts delivered to his vulnerable foe. And, when Richard fell ill after the battle, Salah al-Din sent fresh fruit and water, as well as his personal physician to look after the English monarch.

On September 2, 1192, the two rulers finally signed a treaty that brought five years of peace between the Muslims and the remaining Crusader kingdoms on the coast. Muslims retained control of Jerusalem, but unarmed Christian pilgrims were given the right to pass freely through the territory.

A Continuing Inspiration

Salah al-Din died a year after he and Richard signed their treaty. On his deathbed, the Kurdish general gave his son al-Zahir these instructions:

My son, I commend thee to the most high God. . . . Do His will, for that way lies peace. Abstain from shedding blood . . . for blood that is spilt never sleeps. Seek to win the hearts of thy people, and watch over their prosperity; for it is to secure their happiness that thou art appointed by God and me. Try to gain the hearts of thy ministers, nobles, and emirs. If I have become great it is because I have won men's hearts by kindness and gentleness.

Salah al-Din continues to play an important role in the historical consciousness of modern Muslims. Many consider him a moral example not only because he liberated Jerusalem, but also because he was quite magnanimous toward his enemies, often in spite of their treachery. He is also remembered for always keeping his word, for his generosity to the poor, for his personal piety and sense of self-restraint, for his tolerance of other religions, and for his unwavering chivalry.

 Text-Dependent Questions

1. What were the Crusades? Why were they fought?
2. What is the first thing Salah al-Din did after becoming vizier in 1169?
3. What did Salah al-Din accomplish in 1187?
4. What European ruler led the Third Crusade against the forces of Salah al-Din?

 Research Project

The Crusades were a series of wars waged by European Christians against Muslims for control over the Holy Land (Jerusalem and the surrounding areas where Jesus Christ lived and taught in the first century CE. Crusades were fought between 1095 and 1291, with additional conflicts related to the Christian Byzantine Empire continuing until the mid-15th century. Using your school library, find out more about the Crusades and the Muslim response to them. Choose a topic related to one of the Crusades, such as military campaigns or the economic and social benefits of the interaction between these two civilizations. Write a two-page paper and present it to your class.

6

Malcolm X

When Malcolm X arrived in Saudi Arabia in April 1964, he was detained at the airport in the city of Jedda. Malcolm intended to visit the holy city of Mecca and participate in the soul-cleansing pilgrimage known as the hajj. But only Muslims are allowed to enter the city of the prophet Muhammad's birth, and even though Malcolm carried a letter of introduction from an Islamic scholar in the United States, the authorities in Jedda did not believe Malcolm was a true Muslim. They informed him that he would have to appear before a religious judge and prove his devotion to Islam.

Eighteen years before his arrival in Jedda, Malcolm had joined the Nation of Islam, an African American religious and cultural sect whose members were widely known as Black Muslims. The Nation of Islam borrowed its *ideology* heavily from the Qur'an and Islamic law. Black Muslims, like all Muslims, pray five times a day while facing in the direction of Mecca. However, the Nation of Islam departs from mainstream Islamic doctrine on several points. For example, main-

Opposite: Malcolm X speaks at a rally shortly after his 1964 hajj to Mecca. The trip to Mecca marked a spiritual turning point for the well-known American black activist.

stream Muslims believe that Muhammad is God's final messenger, but members of the Nation of Islam also regard their sect's second leader, Elijah Muhammad, as a messenger of Allah.

Shortly before Malcolm's arrival in Saudi Arabia, Islamic leaders had criticized the Nation of Islam for other reasons. During the 1960s, a time of racial tension in the United States, leaders of the Nation of Islam openly expressed the view that white people are evil. A goal of the Nation of Islam was the creation of a separate black state inside the United States, where African Americans could live under their own authority. Mainstream Muslim leaders recoiled at such notions, claiming they ran counter to the spirit of Islam.

Malcolm wanted to make a religious pilgrimage to Mecca in the hopes of redefining his own beliefs. After joining the Black Muslims, he had become one of the sect's most influential leaders. He was committed to the goals of the Nation of Islam, following Elijah Muhammad with unquestioned loyalty. Eventually, however, Malcolm found himself at odds with Elijah, mostly because of the leader's personal life. In 1964 Malcolm X left the Nation of Islam and founded his own group, which he named the Muslim Mosque Inc. Soon, he was on his way to Saudi Arabia to participate in the hajj.

His attitude and the direction of his life changed even while he was in detention awaiting his hearing before the hajj court. Taken to a *dormitory* with other pilgrims in transit, Malcolm met people of many races and found them friendly and willing to share their food. Elijah Muhammad's warning that all white people were dev-

 ## Words to Understand in This Chapter

dormitory—a large bedroom for a number of people in a school or institution.

ideology—a system of ideas and ideals, especially one that forms the basis of economic or political theory and policy.

The tents of pilgrims stand outside Mina, near Mecca, with the plain of Arafat visible in the distance, in this photo from the mid-1960s. After sharing his pilgrimage experience with Muslims of all races and national backgrounds, Malcolm wrote, "America needs to understand Islam, because this is the one religion that erases from its society the race problem. . . . I have never before seen sincere and true brotherhood practiced by all colors together, irrespective of their color."

ils did not seem to hold true here in the heart of the Islamic world.

"In America, 'white man' meant specific attitudes and actions toward the black man, and toward all other non-white men," Malcolm wrote later in his autobiography. "But in the Muslim world, I had seen that men with white complexions were more genuinely brotherly than anyone else had ever been. That morning was the start of a radical alteration in my whole outlook about 'white' men."

Malcolm was rescued from detention by Saudi friends who vouched for him. He was taken to a private home in Jedda and, the next day, appeared before the hajj court and received permission to make the pilgrimage.

When Malcolm arrived in Mecca, he went first to the Sacred Mosque, where he participated in the ritual circumambulation of the Kaaba. He was awed by the sight of tens of thousands of other pilgrims undertaking the same ritual. On the seventh circuit around the shrine, he prostrated himself in prayer with his head pressed to the ground.

Throughout this experience, he was overwhelmed by the numbers of people of all colors sharing equally in the rituals of Islam. "There were tens of thousands of pilgrims, from all over the world. They were of all colors, from blue-eyed blonds to black-skinned Africans. But we were all participating in the same ritual displaying a spirit of unity and brotherhood that my experiences in America had led me to believe never could exist between the white and the non-white," he wrote. "America needs to understand Islam, because this is the one religion that erases from its society the race problem. Throughout my travels in the Muslim world, I have met, talked to, and even eaten with people who in America would have been considered white—but the 'white' attitude was removed from their minds by the religion of Islam. I have never before seen sincere and true brotherhood practiced by all colors together, irrespective of their color."

Early Life

Malcolm X was born Malcolm Little on May 19, 1925, in Omaha, Nebraska. He was one of eight children of Earl Little, a Baptist minister, and Louise Norton Little, a homemaker. Earl Little's outspokenness in support of civil rights for blacks may have cost him his life. In 1931, after the Littles moved to Lansing, Michigan, Earl's mutilated body was found sprawled across trolley tracks. Police declared his death an accident, but Malcolm could not help but suspect that his father had been killed by whites who sought to silence him.

Louise Little was traumatized by her husband's violent death and overwhelmed by the sudden responsibility of raising eight children on her own. Soon she was committed to a mental institution, and the children were sent to live in foster homes and orphanages. Malcolm found himself in a foster home in Mason,

Michigan, near Lansing. He attended a mixed-race junior high school. Malcolm soon proved himself one of the school's best students—in the eighth grade, he ranked third academically. But at Mason Junior High the young student was exposed to racist attitudes that would sap his willingness to learn and lead him into a life of crime.

Near the end of his eighth-grade year, Malcolm's English teacher, Richard Kaminska, asked the boy whether he had given thought to a career. Yes, Malcolm replied. He told Kaminska he was thinking of pursuing a career in law. "We all like you," Kaminska told him, "but you've got to be realistic about being a nigger. A lawyer—that's no realistic goal for a nigger. You need to think about something you can be. You're good with your hands. Why don't you plan on carpentry?"

Malcolm later said that he was devastated by those words. "I just gave up," he recalled. His commitment to school waned, and he took to cutting classes and hanging around street corners. He bounced from foster home to foster home, finally moving in with an older sister in Boston. There, he turned to petty crime. By 1940, at the age of 15, he was finished with school.

For the next few years, Malcolm (then nicknamed "Detroit Red") lived in Harlem, New York. He found work as a waiter, but mostly he got money through crime. After returning to Boston in 1946, Malcolm stole an expensive diamond-studded wristwatch, then foolishly took it to a jewelry store to be repaired. The jeweler suspected that the watch was stolen and notified police. Malcolm was arrested when he returned to the store to pick up the watch. He pleaded guilty to participating in a string of burglaries and was sentenced to 10 years in prison. He was not yet 21 years old.

Conversion

Central Library, Henry Street,
An Lárleabharlann, Sráid Annra
Tel: 8734333

Malcolm was given a job in the prison furniture shop. He rediscovered books and became a voracious reader, devouring everything in the prison library from Aesop's fables to Shakespeare. To help improve his vocabulary, he copied pages word for word out of the dictionary.

While in prison, Malcolm received a letter from his brother Philbert, announcing that he had joined a new religious sect specifically for blacks called the Nation of Islam. The letter explained the teachings of Elijah Muhammad, including the belief that the world was headed for Judgment Day, when Allah would subdue the whites and deliver the black people from segregation, menial jobs, and lower-class lives. The letter said that Malcolm's brother Reginald had joined the sect as well.

At first Malcolm had little interest in the Nation of Islam, but he soon learned that other inmates were members of the sect. He started listening to what they had to say. When Reginald came to the prison for a visit, he told Malcolm that all white people were "devils." Malcolm thought hard about that message. Wasn't it

Boston police photographs of Malcolm Little, taken after his arrest for larceny in 1946. It was while he was in prison that the young man was first exposed to the Nation of Islam.

true that all the people responsible for the misery in his life were white? The men who murdered his father? His English teacher? The jeweler who turned him in? The police, prosecuting attorney, and judge who sent him to prison? The jailers?

When Reginald left, Malcolm spent several weeks in spiritual self-examination, trying to understand the new direction his life was about to take. "I would sit in my room and stare," he later said. "At the dining room table, I would hardly eat, only drink the water. I nearly starved. Fellow inmates, concerned, and guards, apprehensive, asked what was wrong with me. It was suggested I visit the doctor, and I didn't. . . . I was going through the hardest thing, also the greatest thing, for any human being to do; to accept that which is already within you, and around you."

Rising Star in the Nation of Islam

When Malcolm was released from prison on early parole in 1952, he went to Detroit and moved in with his brother Wilfred. Soon he traveled to Chicago to meet Elijah Muhammad and learn more about the Nation of Islam. During this visit, he dropped the surname Little, believing that the name had been assigned to his enslaved ancestors. Like many other Black Muslims, he adopted the surname X, which symbolized his true family name and the heritage that had been left behind in Africa. "For me, my 'X' replaced the white slavemaster name of 'Little' which some blue-eyed devil named Little had imposed upon my paternal forebears," Malcolm wrote. "The receipt of my 'X' meant that forever after in the Nation of Islam, I would be known as Malcolm X. Mr. Muhammad taught that we would keep this 'X' until God Himself returned and gave us a Holy Name from His own mouth."

Elijah Muhammad saw in Malcolm X a promising young pupil. He recognized Malcolm's magnetism, which he knew would help draw new members to the Nation of Islam. Over the next few years Malcolm would prove to be an electric speaker and organizer who challenged blacks to speak out for their rights. His orations

Elijah Muhammad was the leader of the Nation of Islam when Malcolm Little joined the sect in the early 1950s.

were tinged with a militancy and anger that frightened many whites. It is estimated that during the 11 years Malcolm X recruited members for the Nation of Islam, the sect's membership grew from just a few hundred to about 30,000. It was also during this period that he met his future wife, Betty; the couple would marry and become the parents of five daughters.

Malcolm agreed to spread the word of Elijah Muhammad to different cities. His first assignment was in Boston, where he helped recruit new members and establish a Nation of Islam mosque. Next, he spent several months in Philadelphia working to revitalize a mosque whose membership had eroded as a result of internal squabbling. Finally, he was dispatched to New York City to serve as minister of a Nation of Islam mosque in the country's largest city. "I can't start to describe the welter of emotions," Malcolm said at the time. "For Mr. Muhammad's teachings to really resurrect American black people, Islam obviously had to grow, to grow very big." And, as Malcolm pointed out, with more than a million black people living in its five boroughs, New York City held vast potential for increasing the Nation of Islam's membership.

Malcolm recruited members by stationing himself outside black Christian churches in Harlem. When worshippers poured out of the churches after Sunday morning services, Malcolm would invite them to attend a Nation of Islam service that afternoon. Once he convinced people to see what a Nation of Islam service was all about, he would try to open their eyes with fiery rhetoric, usually denouncing white people for their treatment of blacks.

Soon his message could be heard outside the tiny storefront mosques of the Nation of Islam. He founded *Muhammad Speaks*, the official publication of the Nation of Islam, and added his fiery commentary to the magazine's editorial pages. He wrote newspaper columns and served as a spokesman for the sect, finding himself much in demand by radio and TV interviewers.

This was an era of great social upheaval in American society. In 1955 in Montgomery, Alabama, Rosa Parks refused to give up her seat on a bus to a white man. The incident led to the Montgomery bus boycott, whose leader, Martin Luther King Jr., would rise to national prominence as a civil rights activist. Two years later, in Little Rock, Arkansas, federal troops were called in to protect black students who enrolled in a whites-only high school.

However, Malcolm X and other leaders of the Nation of Islam felt little solidarity with black activists like King, who sought to integrate society and achieve equal rights. The goal of the Black

Muslims, by contrast, was a separate nation within American society—a place where blacks could live on their own, depend on their own labors, educate their own children, and have no contact with white people. Malcolm was ferocious in his criticism of black leaders or groups favoring any sort of accommodation with white society. For example, he labeled the National Association for the Advancement of Colored People (NAACP) a "black body with a white head" and described Martin Luther King as "a chump, not a champ."

Malcolm's uncompromising attitude helped sway many militant blacks to join the Nation of Islam. Clearly, many believed that the efforts of King and others in the civil rights movement were not proceeding quickly enough, and the Nation of Islam offered an alternative.

In 1963, however, Malcolm's incendiary rhetoric came back to haunt him. Nine days after the assassination of President John F. Kennedy—an event that left Americans shocked, stunned, and in mourning—Malcolm delivered a sermon in New York during which he compared Kennedy's murder with the killing, only weeks earlier, of South Vietnam's president in a coup that U.S. officials went along with if not actively supported. In essence, Malcolm said, Kennedy got what was coming to him. "Chickens coming home to roost never did make me sad," he said. "They've always made me glad."

The next day, Malcolm's remarks were reported in newspapers across the country, causing widespread outrage. Elijah Muhammad promptly relieved Malcolm of his duties as head of the New York mosque and ordered him not to speak publicly, deliver sermons, or publish commentaries in the newspapers. Publicly, Malcolm accepted the gag order. Privately, he seethed at Elijah's directive. "I was in a state of emotional shock," Malcolm said later. "My head felt like it was bleeding inside."

The rift between the Nation of Islam's leader and its most prominent spokesman did not originate with Malcolm's ill-advised remarks about the Kennedy assassination. Rather, it had been developing for months. Malcolm had been shocked and disillusioned to learn that, in spite of Elijah Muhammad's continual admonishments that his followers must honor their wives and families, the Nation of Islam leader had been carrying on numerous extramarital affairs and had fathered at least eight children out of wedlock. Malcolm's criticism of Elijah's behavior to other members of the Nation of Islam had increasingly put him at odds with the Nation's leader.

Malcolm X stands on the steps of a courthouse in Queens, New York, where a police brutality case was being heard, 1959. Unlike other civil rights leaders of the 1950s and 1960s, such as Dr. Martin Luther King, Malcolm and the Black Muslims advocated a separate black society within the United States.

Malcolm X addresses a crowd in January 1965. Just a few weeks later he was assassinated while addressing a rally for the Organization of Afro-American Unity.

The Path to Mainstream Islam

Malcolm X officially broke with the Nation of Islam on March 12, 1964, when he announced the formation of the Muslim Mosque Inc. Later that year Malcolm made the hajj to Mecca. He returned to the United States having fully abandoned his black separatist beliefs, and he adopted the Islamic name El-Hajj Malik al-Shabazz to signal his conversion and total commitment to mainstream Islam. "I don't believe in any form of racism," he told his followers. "I don't believe in any form of discrimination. I believe in Islam."

But some Black Muslims were bitter at Malcolm X's denunciations of Elijah Muhammad, and they suspected that his goal was to destroy the Nation of Islam. He received numerous death threats. On February 14, 1965, the Shabazz home in New York

City was firebombed; fortunately, Malcolm and his family escaped. A week later, however, he would not be so lucky.

Malcolm was to deliver a speech at a rally for the Organization of Afro-American Unity, a group he had helped form to promote racial justice. Shortly after he strode onto the stage and uttered the Islamic greeting "*As salaam alaikum,*" three gunmen (later identified as Black Muslims) emerged from the crowd and shot him at point-blank range. Within minutes the 39-year-old—who four decades later remains a hero to many Americans and Muslims—was dead.

Throughout his life, Malcolm X was an articulate, tireless, and uncompromising advocate of racial justice. More than that, though, it is his extraordinary personal journey—from an angry advocate of racial separatism to a person who recognized the kinship of all peoples—that continues to inspire American Muslims, who see in that journey a shining example of the transformative power of their faith.

 Text-Dependent Questions

1. What happened to Malcolm X's father, Earl Little?
2. Why did Malcolm join the Nation of Islam while in prison?
3. For what comment was Malcolm X removed from his position as head of the New York mosque of the Nation of Islam? What was the real reason for his removal?

 Research Project

Compare and contrast the Islamic religion with the Nation of Islam, which was founded in Detroit around 1930. List ways that they are similar, and ways that they are different. Present the list to your class; be prepared to explain the differences in some depth.

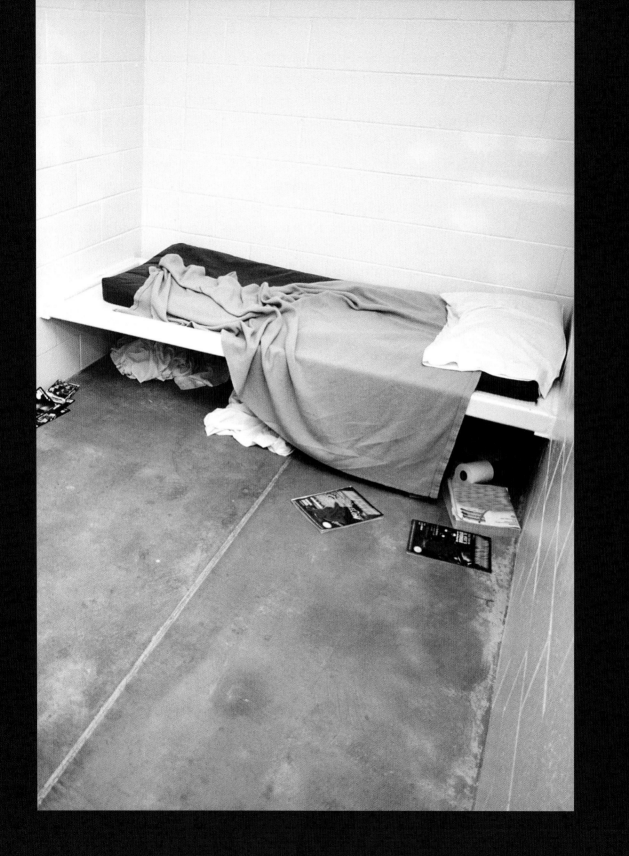

7

Zainab al-Ghazali

At dawn on August 20, 1965, Zainab al-Ghazali awoke to the sounds of men pounding on the door of her home. The intrusion did not come as a shock to the 48-year-old Egyptian woman. She knew that agents for President Gamal Abdel Nasser intended to arrest her. During the previous few weeks, Nasser's agents had arrested many of her friends in the outlawed Muslim Brotherhood. To prepare for her imprisonment, Zainab had already packed a small suitcase.

Zainab opened the door and was confronted by Nasser's agents. They demanded to enter her home. Zainab asked if they had a search warrant.

As Zainab recalled later, the men weren't particularly interested in the niceties of investigative procedure. "Warrant!" they laughed. "What warrant, you fool? We live in the time of [Nasser]. We can do whatever we like to you, you dog!"

Opposite: Zainab al-Ghazali was imprisoned for six years because of her belief that Egypt's government should be based on Islamic principles. In her book *Return of the Pharaoh: Memoir in Nasir's Prison*, she describes how the brutal treatment she faced increased her dedication to Islam.

And with that, they pushed their way into Zainab's home. They searched the house, tearing rooms apart in an attempt to find evidence linking Zainab to the Muslim Brotherhood. They removed books, personal papers, money, and valuables. Finally, they shoved Zainab into the back of a truck. After a short drive, the truck arrived at a military prison in Cairo.

Once inside the prison, she was led past rows of cells where she saw hapless men suspended from the ceiling by their wrists. Zainab heard the sound of whips striking flesh and the cries of pain from the unfortunate victims of the torture.

Eventually Zainab was thrown into a darkened room. She had only a moment to wonder what ordeal was in store for her. Suddenly, a light switch was thrown, and Zainab found herself surrounded by vicious dogs.

"Scared, I closed my eyes and put my hands to my chest," she wrote later. "Within seconds, the snarling dogs were all over me, and I could feel their teeth tearing into every part of my body. Clenching my hands tight into my armpits, I began to recount the names of Allah, beginning with 'O Allah! O Allah!' The dogs were unrelenting, digging their teeth into my scalp, my shoulders, back, chest and wherever another had not already taken hold."

Zainab was locked in the room with the dogs for several hours. Finally, guards entered the room and led the animals away. Zainab's wounds turned out to be minor; she believes her constant prayers to Allah saved her life that first day in prison.

Zainab would spend six long years in Nasser's prisons. She endured many days of torture, starvation, and threats. Her

Words to Understand in This Chapter

flogging—to beat someone with a whip or stick as punishment or torture.

interrogator—a person who aggressively asks questions of someone, especially a suspect or a prisoner), for government or official purposes.

interrogators repeatedly demanded that she admit to crimes she did not commit, particularly a role in a plot to assassinate President Nasser. She steadfastly refused to confess to the false accusations; nor would she give up the names of other members of the Muslim Brotherhood, because she knew they would be arrested and tortured by agents of the Nasser regime.

Zainab survived Nasser's prisons and emerged as an icon for Egyptian Muslims—a true believer in the faith willing to sacrifice her freedom or her life for the future of Islam.

In the Spirit of Nusayba

Zainab al-Ghazali was born on January 2, 1917, the daughter of a prosperous cotton merchant who devoted his free hours to the study of the Qur'an. Shaykh al-Ghazali al-Jabili taught religious classes and preached in mosques, and he instilled in his daughter a love of Islam. From the earliest years of her childhood, Zainab recalled her father telling her that she would become a great leader among the Muslim people. Zainab's father often compared her with Nusayba, a woman from Madina who fought alongside the prophet Muhammad during the Battle of Uhud in the year 625.

Zainab recalled: "He always said to me that, God willing, I would be an Islamic leader. . . . And I would say to him, 'I will be Nusayba.'"

By the time she was 18, Zainab al-Ghazali—guided by the lessons her father taught her—had begun to display her leadership qualities. In 1935 she formed an organization called Jama'at al-Sayyidat al-Muslimat (the Muslim Women's Association), whose goal was to teach Islamic principles to Egyptian women and instruct them in their roles as Muslim wives and mothers. Soon the organization found itself filling a variety of functions: collecting money for poor people, finding jobs for the unemployed, counseling Muslim couples who were experiencing marital difficulties, establishing an orphanage.

The Muslim Women's Association also had a political arm.

Zainab and the group's other leaders were committed to seeing Egypt become an Islamic state.

The Muslim Women's Association soon came to the attention of Hasan al-Banna, founder and leader of al-Ikhwan al-Muslimun (the Muslim Brotherhood). The Brotherhood, established in 1928 in the city of Ismailia, had grown into an influential organization.

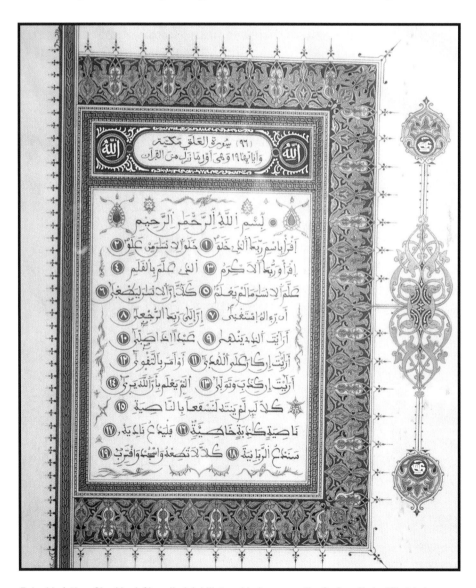

Zainab's father, Shaykh al-Ghazali al-Jabili, taught classes on the Qur'an. He instilled in her a love for her faith and encouraged her to take a leadership role.

Its principal goal was to establish an Egyptian government that would be guided by the Qur'an and Sunna—a goal shared by the leadership of the Muslim Women's Association. The Brotherhood was also committed to ridding Egypt of foreign, and especially British, influence.

Al-Banna hoped to involve women in his movement, but efforts by the Muslim Brotherhood to organize Egyptian women met with only limited success. By 1937, when the Brotherhood is believed to have had a membership of 500,000, the associated "Muslim Sisters" included only about 5,000 women. Most of them served as teachers in schools that had been established by the Brotherhood.

Al-Banna approached Zainab al-Ghazali and asked her to merge the Muslim Women's Association into the Muslim Brotherhood. Zainab believed fully in al-Banna's vision for the future of Egypt. Still, folding the Women's Association into the Brotherhood was not an action she could take on her own. Zainab had to present the proposal to the General Assembly of the Muslim Women's Association. She did so, but the members of the General Assembly were unconvinced; they suggested that the two groups simply work together in pursuit of the same goals. But al-Banna insisted on a total union.

For the next dozen years, Zainab al-Ghazali and Hasan al-Banna met repeatedly and discussed their common goals. Finally, in early 1949, Zainab agreed to merge the Muslim Women's Association into the Brotherhood. "I pledge allegiance to you for the establishment of the Islamic state," she told him. "The least I can give for this, is shedding my blood and merging the Muslim ladies' group with the Ikhwan."

But the merger would never take place. On the night of February 12, 1949, as Zainab left for a meeting with al-Banna, she received word that the Brotherhood leader had been gunned down on a Cairo street. The killers turned out to be agents of Ibrahim Abd al-Hadi, Egypt's prime minister. Al-Hadi's government soon outlawed the Muslim Brotherhood.

In 1952 a revolutionary group in the Egyptian army, known as the Free Officers, deposed Egypt's King Farouk I and seized power. The ideals of the Free Officers included social equality and progressive, democratic government. But as one of their members, Gamal Abdel Nasser, vested all power in himself, the reality was somewhat different. An enormously popular figure in the Arab world, at home Nasser was intolerant and repressive. He frequently dealt with critics and political opponents through arrest, torture, and even killing.

Nasser envisioned a secular society and government for Egypt, which went against the goals of the Muslim Brotherhood. In 1954 a member of the Brotherhood attempted to assassinate the Egyptian leader, spurring Nasser to order a ruthless new crackdown on the group and its followers. From that moment until Nasser's death in 1970, the Brotherhood was under continual pressure from the government.

A Leader in the Muslim Brotherhood

During the 1950s, in the face of the official persecution, the Brotherhood existed as an underground organization. Three members emerged as the society's leaders in this period: Sayyid Qutb, a poet, writer, and literary critic; Abd al-Fattah Ismail, who had been a loyal aide to al-Banna; and Zainab al-Ghazali.

By then Zainab was a prominent figure in Egyptian society. Her first husband was a wealthy and influential man, but she divorced him because he frowned on her political activity.

"I found that [my first] marriage took up all my time and kept me from my mission, and my husband did not agree with my work," she recalled. "I had made a condition that if we had any major disagreements we would separate, and the Islamic cause was essential."

Zainab soon married again. Her second husband, al-Hajj Muhammad Salim Salim, proved much more willing to accept her work.

This was a dangerous time for anyone associated with the Muslim Brotherhood, as Nasser's agents were constantly on the lookout for members of the outlawed society. Qutb was arrested and imprisoned many times. Still, the Brotherhood managed to increase its influence.

Meanwhile, Zainab continued her duties as head of the Muslim Women's Association. The organization published an influential magazine, and Zainab used its pages to support the establishment of an Islamic state.

In 1962 leaders of the Muslim Brotherhood formulated a plan they hoped would culminate in the establishment of an Islamic state in Egypt. For the next 13 years, members of the Muslim Brotherhood planned to reach out to all Egyptians and train them in the laws of Islam. At the end of the 13 years, the Brotherhood

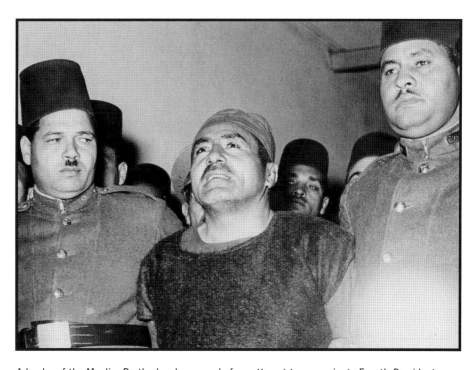

A leader of the Muslim Brotherhood, accused of an attempt to assassinate Egypt's President Nasser, is escorted from his prison cell to the execution chamber of Cairo Prison, December 1954. After the attempt on his life Nasser cracked down on the Brotherhood, making the organization illegal and arresting many of its leaders.

would conduct a national survey of Egyptians, asking if they agreed with the notion that the country should be governed according to the Qur'an. If 75 percent of the population supported the establishment of an Islamic state, the Brotherhood would rise up and demand that the Egyptian constitution be abolished and the Qur'an installed as the law of the land.

Zainab and the other leaders of the Brotherhood never had the opportunity to see their education program fulfilled. In 1964, soon after Sayyid Qutb was released from prison, Nasser's agents reported to the president that the Muslim Brotherhood leader was planning to organize a military arm. Nasser immediately ordered a new crackdown. During the next two years, some 100,000 members of the society were arrested and thrown into prison. Qutb and Ismail were taken into custody in 1965. Zainab al-Ghazali's arrest came that year as well.

Prisoner of the Nasser Regime

For the first year of her imprisonment, the torture would be unrelenting. In their quest to break Zainab's spirit, get her to confess to crimes she had not committed, and force her to betray other members of the Muslim Brotherhood, Nasser's jailers were merciless. There were repeated *floggings* and attacks by dogs. One punishment cell was flooded. For nine days, Zainab was forced to sit alone in the cell, submerged up to her chin in rancid water. The water stung and infected her open wounds.

Zainab regularly found herself in the prison hospital, where her wounds were treated but never allowed to completely heal. She received just enough medical care so that she could be returned to her cell for more torture.

And always, the interrogators wanted her to admit to participating in a plot to murder President Nasser. They told her that if she would tell them about the plot and name the other conspirators, they would release her and even see to it that she was awarded a job in the government.

"I was asked about certain people, and each time I said I did not know them I was tortured," she said.

Finally, after nearly two years of torture and interrogation, Zainab was told she would have to stand trial. The trial was a farce. In the courtroom, Zainab sat in a cage while a prosecuting attorney laid out a fabricated case against her. The judge was obviously not impartial; whenever Zainab tried to speak in her own defense, she was told by the judge to keep quiet.

Ultimately, Zainab received a sentence of 25 years in prison at hard labor. More than 40 other members of the Brotherhood had also gone on trial with Zainab. Many of their sentences were even harsher. Sayyid Qutb and Abd al-Fattah Ismail each received the death penalty, and their sentences were promptly carried out. Zainab called them "martyrs for the sake of Allah."

Three weeks after Zainab's sentence was handed down, she heard the news that her husband had died, most likely from a heart condition. Following Zainab's arrest, Nasser's agents had robbed Salim Salim of his money, land, and other property and forced him to sign papers divorcing his wife.

As for Zainab, she was transferred to a woman's prison. She recalled that her move to al-Qanatir Prison occurred on June 5, 1967, just as Nasser's troops were suffering a humiliating defeat at the hands of the Israelis in the Six-Day War. That's not what the prisoners were told, though. Zainab said soldiers boasted to her that President Nasser achieved a great victory and that his regime was stronger than ever. One of the soldiers started beating Zainab, declaring, "We've won, we've won despite you, and your hour has come right now."

The truth was, of course, much different. Not only did Egypt lose decisively in the 1967 war with Israel, but Nasser's troops had for years suffered huge losses in the civil war in North Yemen, where the Egyptian president was backing insurgents. Humiliated by the Israelis and worn down by the Yemenis, Nasser's military was bankrupt and in a shambles. Finally, the Egyptians left North Yemen in October 1967.

Following the twin fiascoes of the Six-Day War and the war in North Yemen, Nasser held onto power for three more years. He died of a heart attack in 1970 and was succeeded by his vice president, Anwar al-Sadat.

Freedom

Sadat released many of the political prisoners imprisoned by Nasser, including Zainab al-Ghazali. After four years in al-Qanatir Prison, and a total of six years behind bars, Zainab was called into the warden's office and informed that she had been freed by order of President Sadat.

Zainab left prison on August 10, 1971, her body worn down by six years of imprisonment, torture, and hard labor. Her mind was as sharp as ever, though, and even as she walked through the gates to freedom, she resolved to continue speaking out for an Islamic state as long as breath remained in her body.

"The establishment of an Islamic state is an obligation on Muslims and their equipment for it is the call to Allah in the same manner the Prophet, peace be upon him, and his companions called to Him," she said. "This is the mission of every Muslim, whether they are from the [Muslim Brotherhood] or not."

Zainab al-Ghazali died on August 3, 2005. However, the Muslim Brotherhood continued its work in Egypt. During January 2011, Egyptians began to hold mass demonstrations aimed at removing Sadat's successor, Hosni Mubarak, from power. Unable to stop the protests, Mubarak resigned and fled the country in February 2011. Egypt's military governed the country for six months, until elections could be held.

In the first national elections, held in June 2012, Mohamed Morsi was elected president. Morsi was a leader of the Muslim Brotherhood who, like Zainab, had been imprisoned by the Egyptian government. It appeared that the dream of an Islamic government in Egypt could be achieved. But the Muslim Brotherhood and the Egyptian military soon clashed over the future of the country. Morsi was criticized for trying to extend his powers as president, and some Egyptians became disillusioned because his government was not as democratic as they had hoped. By June 2013, Egyptians were demonstrating in the streets again, this time calling for Morsi to be removed from office. The military removed Morsi the following month in a coup d'état led by General Abdel Fattah el-Sisi. Morsi's supporters protested his removal, but the military cracked down on dissent. Eventually, the military-backed interim government banned the Muslim Brotherhood again.

Despite this, Egyptian Islamists will undoubtedly continue to follow the example of Zainab al-Ghazali and others, who showed courage and resolve in standing up for their faith.

 # Text-Dependent Questions

1. What organization did Zainab al-Ghazali establish in 1935? What were this organization's goals?
2. Who founded the Muslim Brotherhood?
3. Why was Zainab al-Ghazali arrested in 1965? How long did she spend in prison?

 # Research Project

Anwar el-Sadat, who freed Zainab al-Ghazali from prison in 1971, was an important Egyptian leader of the 20th century. Although he reversed some of Nasser's harsh policies toward islamists like Zainab, he did not permit the Muslim Brotherhood to operate openly, and he also angered many in the Arab world by making a peace treaty with the State of Israel in 1979. Sadat was assassinated two years later, with the murderer shouting "death to Pharaoh"—a reference to the president as an abusive secular leader, similar to the title of Zainab's book criticizing Nasser, *Return of the Pharaoh.* Do some research on Sadat using the Intenet or your school library, and write a two-page paper about his attitudes toward and treatment of Islamists during his time in power.

8

Mecca and Other Holy Places

Throughout the history of Islam, Muslims have held great reverence for the city of Mecca. "Turn then thy face in the direction of the Sacred Mosque; wherever ye are, turn your faces in that direction!" the Qur'an instructs Muslims when they pray. Five times each day, more than a billion Muslims face Mecca when they say their prayers.

Mecca, which sits in an *arid* valley on the Arabian Peninsula some 50 miles east of the Red Sea, was an important commercial and religious city long before Muhammad's birth around 570 CE. Its economic importance was due primarily to its location; Mecca was a familiar stop on the caravan trade routes because travelers knew the city contained an abundant source of water—a well known as Zamzam.

Although it is the spiritual heart of Islam, Mecca has been controlled by many different empires and rulers throughout history. It was captured by the Egyptians in the 13th century; control of the city

Opposite: The Dome of the Rock, located on the site of the ancient Jewish temple in Jerusalem, is the oldest Muslim shrine in existence, built in 691. Muslims consider Jerusalem to be a sacred city, just as Jews and Christians do.

passed to the Ottoman Turks in the early 16th century. From 1517 to 1916 the city was ruled on behalf of the Turkish sultan by the *sharifs*, who were members of the Hashimite clan (and therefore descendants of Muhammad). In 1916, during the First World War, the Turks were driven out of Mecca by Arab forces led by Sharif Hussein ibn Ali, who worked with British troops. After the war ended, Sharif Hussein became the first king of the Hijaz, but this kingdom on the Arabian Peninsula was short lived. In 1924 the city was occupied by Abd al-Aziz ibn Saud, who eventually conquered a large part of the peninsula and established the modern state of Saudi Arabia. Mecca today is located in Saudi Arabia; it is the religious capital of the country.

The city of Mecca has changed tremendously throughout its history. In fact, Muslims say that Mecca has changed so much just in the past 50 years that it is practically unrecognizable. New hotels, some of them very luxurious, are constantly being built; these host the Muslims who make pilgrimages to Mecca each year. In addition, Mecca is crisscrossed with vast, wide freeways, and its skyline includes many new high-rise buildings.

Although the government of Saudi Arabia, where Mecca is located, uses its vast oil wealth to maintain the roads, utilities, and infrastructure of the holy city, Mecca is free from the industrial sites, such as *petrochemical* plants and oil production facilities, that can be found in most of the kingdom's other cities. There is commerce in Mecca, to be sure; many of the city's 550,000 permanent residents make their livings catering to the more than 2 million pilgrims who visit al-Masjid al-Haram, the Sacred Mosque (or Great Mosque of Mecca), each year.

 Words to Understand in This Chapter

arid—a climate that receives little or no rain or precipitation, and is too dry to support vegetation.

petrochemical—substances obtained by the refining and processing of petroleum or natural gas.

The Religious Significance of Mecca

All Muslims have a duty to make at least one pilgrimage to Mecca during their lifetime, if they can afford it and are physically capable. This pilgrimage is known as the hajj, and it occurs during Dhu al-Hijja, the 12th month of the Islamic lunar calendar. For Muslims, participation in the rituals of the hajj can be a life-altering experience that confirms their faith in Allah.

Because so many pilgrims wish to visit Mecca each year, the Saudi government now regulates the number of Muslims it will admit annually from each country. Those who want to make the pilgrimage must apply. Only Muslims may enter Mecca; non-Muslims are prohibited from visiting the holy city.

The pilgrims' ultimate destination is the ancient Kaaba, which is located in an enormous courtyard of the Great Mosque of

The Great Mosque of Mecca has been expanded many times over the centuries. Today it can hold more than 800,000 people during the hajj. Visitors pray in the direction of the Kaaba, the ancient shrine that is located within the mosque.

Mecca. Muslims believe Adam, the first man, originally built this structure as a place of worship. Tradition holds that the Kaaba is located at the center of the earth. According to legend the building was destroyed in the biblical Great Flood. Around 1900 BCE, Abraham—who is revered by Muslims, Christians, and Jews— came to the Kaaba and rebuilt it with the help of his older son, Ishmael.

The Kaaba sits atop a floor of polished marble tiles that covers nearly 200,000 square feet. The outside of the ancient building is draped with black fabric; there is nothing inside. An ancient black stone, called al-Hajar al-Aswad, is located in the eastern wall of the Kaaba. Muslims consider the black stone a symbolic representation of the effect of sin on the human heart. In Muslim mythology the stone, which came from heaven (it may have been a meteorite), was originally white. It was sent from Allah to Abraham and Ishmael, who were rebuilding the Kaaba, and they placed it in the eastern

Pilgrims to Mecca wear white robes during the hajj to signify their purity and their unity with other Muslims.

wall. From the effect of the sins of humans throughout the ages, the stone became black. (There are other stories surrounding the stone, but they are not central to Muslim dogma and belief.) One of the hajj rituals involves walking around the Kaaba seven times; pilgrims use the stone as a marker to determine how many circuits they have made. After circling the Kaaba seven times, some pilgrims kiss the stone.

The Great Mosque that surrounds the Kaaba has been enlarged many times over the centuries. The original oblong mosque was erected in the eighth century. Today the mosque is many times larger, covering nearly 1.5 million square feet. A total of 64 gates provide entry to what is one of the largest houses of worship in the world—it can hold up to 1 million worshippers. Seen from the air, the mosque resembles an enormous latchkey, with one long arm leading into an octagonal configuration that surrounds the Kaaba. Seven minarets rise high above the mosque into the sky.

That the Great Mosque was changed and enlarged many times is not unusual. Throughout Islamic history, mosques were often expanded, particularly when new ruling dynasties took power. Different empires and dynasties often either paid for improvements to existing structures or commissioned completely new mosques. This was done to bolster the legitimacy of the new rulers with Muslims across the globe.

One of the most prominent features of the Great Mosque is the Mas'aa, a track that represents the path that Hagar, the mother of Ishmael, took between the hills of Safa and Marwa in a frantic search for water for her son. Seven times Hagar ran between the two hills; to commemorate her journey, pilgrims make the journey through the Mas'aa seven times. This reminds the Muslims of God's miraculous intervention to save Hagar and Ishmael, and His creation of the well at Zamzam. Tradition calls for Muslims to make the walk at a brisk pace, but now the path is enclosed against the elements, air-conditioned, and decorated with mosaic tiles. The Zamzam well is located within the Great Mosque, as is the Hijr, believed to be the burial place of Hagar and Ishmael.

Madina

Madina—city of the Prophet—is situated on a fertile plateau where residents cultivate dates and a rich variety of vegetables. The early Muslim community grew and flourished in Madina; Muhammad died in the city and is buried there, as are some of Islam's most important early leaders and caliphs. Because of the city's significance, most Muslims regard Madina as Islam's second-holiest city (some rank it third, behind Mecca and Jerusalem). Like Mecca, Madina is off-limits to non-Muslim travelers, though certain hotels on the outskirts of the city will accept non-Muslim guests.

Muhammad's tomb is located under the so-called Green Dome, constructed by the 19th-century Ottoman sultan Mahmud

The Prophet Muhammad's tomb is located under the green dome of this mosque in Madina. The city in Saudi Arabia remains an important religious center.

II (1808–1839) and reconstructed in 1860 by his successor, Sultan Abd al-Majid I (1839–1861). The dome is at the center of the Masjid al-Nabi (the Prophet's Mosque). From each corner of this mosque tall minarets rise into the sky.

After Muhammad's death, the Islamic empire expanded rapidly into other lands. During the rule of the first three caliphs, Madina remained the political center of Islam. Ali moved the seat of his government to Kufa, and after the death of the fourth caliph and the ascension of the Umayyad dynasty of rulers, the government was moved to Damascus. Thereafter Madina remained more important for religious, rather than political, reasons. Today the city has a permanent population of about 600,000 people.

Jerusalem

The importance of Jerusalem in Islamic theology dates from an event that occurred not long after Allah first revealed Himself to Muhammad. According to a legend, one night the Prophet was awakened by angels and led to the Kaaba. There they were met by a winged, horse-like animal called al-Buraq, which flew the Prophet to Jerusalem. Landing on the ruins of the ancient Jewish temple, Muhammad dismounted and prayed. Muhammad was offered drinks from vessels of wine and milk; when he chose the milk, the angel Gabriel told him, "You have chosen the true religion."

Then the Prophet, accompanied by Gabriel, ascended to heaven, where Muhammad received the command to pray five times a day. He also met with earlier prophets and messengers like Abraham, Moses, and Jesus. The story of Muhammad's Night Journey (known by Muslims as Laylat al-Isra' and al-Miraj) is mentioned in sura 17 of the Qur'an and expounded on at some length in the Hadith. From the early days of Islam, therefore, Muslims have considered Jerusalem a holy city. In fact, after the Night Journey, Muhammad initially told his followers to pray facing Jerusalem rather than Mecca. Muslims call the city al-Quds, an Arabic word that means "the Holy." It is worth noting that Arab

Christians also call the city by the same name.

The most important Muslim shrine in Jerusalem is al-Masjid al-Aqsa (the Aqsa Mosque), which includes the famous Dome of the Rock. This was built over a rock on which Muslims believe Muhammad stood for his ascent to heaven. Muslims believe that the faithful can see Muhammad's footprints embedded in the rock. The ornate dome, completed in 691, is perhaps the oldest extant Islamic monument.

Although Jerusalem has frequently been the site of conflict, the city has a long and rich history. For hundreds of years it was a center of trade, culture, and intellectual exchange in the region. In addition to its significance to Muslims, Jerusalem is very important to followers of the two earlier monotheistic faiths, Judaism and Christianity. King David ruled a powerful Israelite kingdom from Jerusalem around 1000 BCE, and the city has always been an important part of the Jewish religion. Christians also view Jerusalem as a holy city because the crucifixion and resurrection of Jesus occurred there around 29 CE, and it was an early center of Christianity.

Arab Muslims took control of Jerusalem during the rule of the second caliph, Umar ibn al-Khattab (634–644). After that, Christians and Muslims periodically fought over the city. The series of European invasions called the Crusades (1095–1291), for example, were undertaken in part to gain control of Jerusalem. The Ottoman Turks took control of Jerusalem in the 14th century, and it was part of their empire until World War I, when it was captured by British and Arab forces. After the war, the region known as Palestine, which includes Jerusalem, came under the administration of the British.

After the Second World War, the newly formed United Nations presented a plan to divide Palestine into two new states, one Jewish and one Arab. Because of its importance to so many people, Jerusalem was to be administered by the United Nations as an international city that would be open to all. However, the Arab countries and the Palestinians declared their opposition to the

Although most Westerners know that Jerusalem is central to the Jewish faith, few understand the city's significance to Muslims. The Dome of the Rock shrine, and the nearby al-Aqsa Mosque (pictured), are among the most sacred sites in Islam.

U.N. partition plan, and the plan was never implemented. In May 1948, right after the British withdrew from Palestine, the modern state of Israel was declared. Israel was immediately attacked by the armies of five of its Arab neighbors, but the Jewish state managed to survive. By early 1949, when the fighting ended, Israel controlled more than half of Jerusalem; Jordan controlled the Old City and East Jerusalem, along with the territory known as the West Bank.

In June 1967 Israel launched a preemptive strike against Egypt, Syria, and Jordan, in the process capturing East Jerusalem and the Old City. Since then, Muslims have denounced what they consider

The shrine of Fatima Masumeh, sister of the eighth Shiite imam, is located in Qum, Iran. It is considered one of the most sacred Shiite shrines. The building was originally built in the 10th century, and has been expanded and renovated many times, most recently in 2014-15.

Israel's illegal occupation of the city, and control of East Jerusalem and the site of the Aqsa Mosque has been a key issue in Israeli-Palestinian violence, particularly since September 2000.

Cities Important to Shiites

A number of cities are considered holy or significant by Shiites but not necessarily by Sunni Muslims. Many of these are located in Iran and Iraq, where most of the people follow Shiism.

One religiously important city is Karbala, which is located in modern-day Iraq about 65 miles southwest of Baghdad. "Kar'bala" is derived from an Arabic phrase, "*qurb allah*," meaning "Nearness of God." Karbala was the site of the battle in which the Prophet's grandson Hussain was killed in 680. Shiites believe

Hussain sacrificed himself to show that rule by military force is evil, and they revere Karbala as the place of his martyrdom. Hussain's tomb, along with a graveyard where his followers are buried, is among the holy sites in Karbala.

Another city in Iraq that is holy to Shiites is An Najaf, about 100 miles south of Baghdad, where Ali ibn Abi Talib is believed to be buried. Next to the shrine is a cemetery known as Wadi al-Salam ("Valley of Peace"). With 70,000 graves, Wadi al-Salam is the world's second-largest cemetery (Arlington National Cemetery in Virginia, the largest, has more than 90,000 graves).

The name of the city is derived from the Arabic word for "dried river." It is said that a son of Noah drowned while sitting on a mountain in An Najaf after refusing to enter the ark. After the waters of the Great Flood receded, the mountain crumbled and was replaced by a river, but eventually the waters of the river dried up, leaving a dry riverbed.

The city of Qum, Iran, has long been a center for Shiite worship. In the ninth century its inhabitants turned to the Shiite leader Imam Hassan Asger to deliver them from an evil overseer. In Qum, Shiites worship in the magnificently domed Holy Shrine of Fatima, named for the daughter of Muhammad and wife of Ali. Shiite Muslims believe that three of the eight gates of heaven open toward Qum.

 # Text-Dependent Questions

1. Who do Muslims believe originally built the Kaaba in modern-day Mecca? For what purpose was it built?
2. In what Saudi Arabian city is the tomb of the Prophet Muhammad located?
3. What is the most important Muslim shrine in Jerusalem?

 # Research Project

The Battle of Karbala in 680 was a major event in the division of Muslim into Sunni and Shia sects. To understand why the city is revered today by Shiites, read the online article "Karbala: History's Long Shadow," from the BBC. It can be found at http://www.bbc.com/news/world-middle-east-22657029.

Chronology

ca. 570 Muhammad is born in Mecca.

600 Ali ibn Abi Talib is born in Mecca.

610 Muhammad receives the first Qur'anic revelation.

622 The Hijra, or migration from Mecca to Madina, occurs.

630 Mecca surrenders to Muhammad, and Islam becomes the dominant religion on the Arabian Peninsula.

632 Muhammad dies in Mecca; Abu Bakr is selected as the first caliph.

634 Umar is chosen as the second caliph.

644 Uthman becomes the third caliph on the death of Umar; during his reign an authoritative copy of the Qur'an is compiled.

656 Ali is chosen as the fourth caliph; his supporters defeat an army loyal to Ayesha, the Prophet's daughter, at the Battle of the Camel.

657 The Battle of Siffin ends in stalemate when Ali's army refuses to fight against the rebellious army of Muawiya because they have placed passages from the Qur'an on the ends of their spears.

661 Ali is assassinated by a Kharijite; Muawiya assumes the caliphate.

680 Muawiya names his son Yazid to succeed him as caliph, inaugurating the hereditary Umayyad dynasty; Hussain, the younger son of Ali, and a group of his followers are massacred by Yazid's soldiers at Karbala.

685 Work is begun on the Dome of the Rock in Jerusalem, at the place where Muhammad is said to have ascended to heaven on his Night Journey.

717 The Sufi mystic and saint Rabia al-Adawiyya is born in Basra.

750 The Umayyad dynasty is forced from power and the Abbasids take control of the Islamic empire.

Chronology

801	Rabia al-Adawiyya dies.
909	The Fatimid dynasty of rulers, which follows the Ismaili sect of Shiism, comes to power in Egypt.
1095	Pope Urban calls on European Christians to embark on a military campaign against Muslims living in the Holy Land.
1099	The Crusaders capture Jerusalem and establish four Christian kingdoms along the Mediterranean coast.
1138	Salah al-Din Yusuf ibn Ayyub (known in the West as Saladin) is born in Syria.
1169	Salah al-Din is appointed vizier of Egypt.
1174	Salah al-Din conquers Damascus, taking the first step toward unification of the Muslim people.
1187	Salah al-Din captures Jerusalem, returning the city to Islamic rule.
1192	Salah al-Din and King Richard I of England sign a peace treaty that effectively ends the Third Crusade.
1193	Salah al-Din dies.
1902	Abd al-Aziz ibn Saud captures Riyadh.
1916	Sharif Hussein ibn Ali, the emir of Mecca, and his sons lead the Great Arab Revolt against the Ottomans during World War I.
1917	Zainab al-Ghazali is born in Egypt.
1924	Sharif Hussein is ousted as ruler of the Hijaz by Abd al-Aziz ibn Saud.
1925	Malcolm Little is born in Omaha, Nebraska, on May 19.
1927	Hasan al-Banna founds the Egyptian Muslim Brotherhood in the Egyptian city of Ismailia.
1932	Abd al-Aziz ibn Saud establishes the Kingdom of Saudi Arabia.

Chronology

1946 Malcolm Little is sent to prison; while there he learns about the Nation of Islam.

1947 The United Nations votes to partition Palestine into Jewish and Palestinian Arab states.

1948 Israel declares its independence on May 14 and is attacked by Syria, Egypt, Iraq, Transjordan, and Lebanon.

1952 Malcolm Little meets Nation of Islam leader Elijah Muhammad and changes his name to Malcolm X.

1963 Malcolm X is removed from his duties as head of the New York mosque.

1964 Malcolm X officially breaks with the Nation of Islam on March 12; he makes the hajj to Mecca in April, where he gains a greater understanding of mainstream Islamic principles.

1965 On February 21, Malcolm X is shot to death by three gunmen with links to the Nation of Islam.

1967 In June Israel launches a surprise attack on Egypt, Syria, and Jordan, capturing East Jerusalem and the West Bank, Gaza Strip, Sinai Peninsula, and Golan Heights during six days of fighting.

1970 Egyptian leader Gamal Abdel Nasser dies and Anwar al-Sadat becomes president of Egypt.

1971 Zainab al-Ghazali is released from prison.

1993 After secret negotiations in Oslo, Norway, representatives of Israel and the Palestinians establish a framework for an end to violence and the eventual establishment of an autonomous Palestinian state.

2000 The Israeli-Palestinian peace process fails, and the al-Aqsa intifada erupts in the West Bank and Gaza Strip.

Chronology

2006 Pope Benedict XVI inadvertently angers many Muslims with his comments during a speech in Germany; the pope later calls for greater dialogue between Muslims and Christians.

2005 The Fiqh Council of North America issues a *fatwa* condemning terrorism and religious extremism. Zainab al-Ghazali dies on August 3.

2012 Mohamed Morsi, a member of the Muslim Brotherhood, is sworn in as president after he wins Egypt's first competitive presidential election. Morsi would be ousted in June of the following year by a military coup.

2014 In June, the Islamic State of Iraq and the Levant (ISIL) declares a caliphate in the territory they control, stretching from Aleppo in northwestern Syria to the eastern Iraqi province of Diyala. They rename their group Islamic State (IS), although most Western observers continue to refer to the group as ISIL.

2015 In September, more than 2,200 hajj pilgrims are crushed to death by a surging crowd during the "stoning of the devil" ritual at Mina, Saudi Arabia. It is the deadliest hajj disaster in history.

2016 Tensions between Iran and Saudi Arabia rise after King Salman orders the execution of a Shiite cleric, Nimr al-Nimr, along with 46 other dissidents.

Series Glossary

BCE **and** CE—alternatives to the traditional Western designation of calendar eras, which used the birth of Jesus as a dividing line. BCE stands for "Before the Common Era," and is equivalent to BC ("Before Christ"). Dates labeled CE, or "Common Era," are equivalent to Anno Domini (AD, or "the Year of Our Lord").

Hadith—the body of customs, sayings, and traditions ascribed to the prophet Muhammad and his closest companions in the early Muslim community, as recorded by those who witnessed them.

hajj—the fifth pillar of Islam; a pilgrimage to Mecca, which all Muslims who are able are supposed to make at least once in their lifetime.

imam—a Muslim spiritual leader. In the Sunni tradition, an imam is a religious leader who leads the community in prayer. In the Shiite tradition, an imam is a descendant of Muhammad who is the divinely chosen and infallible leader of the community.

jihad—struggle. To Muslims, the "greater jihad" refers to an individual's struggle to live a pure life, while the "lesser jihad" refers to defensive struggle or warfare against oppression and the enemies of Islam.

Qur'an—Islam's holy scriptures, which contain Allah's revelations to the prophet Muhammad in the early seventh century.

Sharia—a traditional system of Islamic law based on the Qur'an, the opinion of Islamic leaders, and the desires of the community.

Shia—one of the two major sects of Islam; members of this sect are called Shiites.

Sufism—a mystical tradition that emphasizes the inner aspect of spirituality through meditation and remembrance of God.

Sunna—the traditions of the prophet Muhammad as exemplified by his actions and words, and preserved in the Qur'an and Hadith.

Sunni—the largest sect of Islam; the name is derived from the Arabic phrase "the Path," referring to those who follow the instructions of Muhammad as recorded in the Qur'an and other ancient writings or traditions.

umma—the worldwide community of Muslims.

Further Reading

Armstrong, Karen. *Muhammad: A Prophet for Our Time*. New York: HarperCollins, 2007.

Aslan, Reza. *No god but God: The Origins, Evolution, and Future of Islam*. New York: Random House, 2011.

al-Ghazali, Zainab. *Return of the Pharaoh: Memoir in Nasir's Prison*. Leicester, England: The Islamic Foundation, 1994.

Harris, Sam, and Maajid Nawaz. *Islam and the Future of Tolerance: A Dialogue*. Cambridge, Mass.: Harvard University Press, 2015.

Hazleton, Lesley. *After the Prophet: The Epic Story of the Shia-Sunni Split in Islam*. New York: Doubleday, 2010.

Hindley, Geoffrey. *Saladin: Hero of Islam*. South Yorkshire, UK: Pen and Sword Books, 2010.

Malcolm X, with Alex Haley. *The Autobiography of Malcolm X*. New York: Grove Press, 1965.

Mansfield, Peter. *A History of the Middle East*. 4th ed. revised and updated by Nicholas Pelham. New York: Penguin Books, 2013.

Seyyed, Hossein Nasr, Sewed H. Nasr, and Ali Kazuyoshi Nomachi. *Mecca the Blessed, Medina the Radiant: The Holiest Cities of Islam*. New York: Aperture, 1997.

Smith, Margaret. *Rabia the Mystic and Her Fellow Saints of Islam*. Cambridge, England: Cambridge University Press, 1984.

Wickham, Carrie Rosefsky. *The Muslim Brotherhood: Evolution of an Islamist Movement*. Princeton: Princeton University Press, 2013.

Leabharlanna Poibli Chathair Baile Átha Cliath

Dublin City Public Libraries

Internet Resources

http://islam.com

A portal with information about Islam, including discussion forums, articles, and links to other resources.

https://sacredsites.com/middle_east/iran/shia_islam.html

An essay on the history of holy places in Islam, and how Muslims of different sects treat such shrines.

http://www.fordham.edu/halsall/islam/islamsbook.html

Fordham University provides this online Islamic History Sourcebook, with links to texts from every period in the history of Islam, as well as maps and other resources.

http://www.mwlusa.org

The website of the Los Angeles–based Muslim Women's League includes essays about the role of women in Islam.

http://daralislam.org

The website of Dar al Islam, a non-profit organization that promotes understanding between Muslims and non-Muslims in the United States. Includes recent news and academic articles on Islamic politics, culture, and history.

http://www.cair.com/

The Council on American-Islamic Relations (CAIR) is an organization dedicated to providing an Islamic perspective on issues of importance to the American people.

Publisher's Note: The websites listed on this page were active at the time of publication. The publisher is not responsible for websites that have changed their address or discontinued operation since the date of publication. The publisher reviews and updates the websites each time the book is reprinted.

Index

Numbers in **bold italic** refer to captions.

Index

Index

Index

Picture Credits

Page

1:    used under license from Shutterstock, Inc.
4:    used under license from Shutterstock, Inc.
8:    Brand X Pictures
10:   Library of Congress
14:   S. M. Amin/Saudi Aramco World/PADIA
17:   Tor Eigeland/Saudi Aramco World/PADIA
18:   Historical photos collection/Saudi Aramco World/PADIA
19:   Tor Eigeland /Saudi Aramco World/PADIA
21:   Brynn Bruijn/Saudi Aramco World/PADIA
23:   Hikrcn / Shutterstock.com
24:   Erich Lessing/Art Resource, NY
28:   S. M. Amin/Saudi Aramco World/PADIA
29:   Erich Lessing/Art Resource, NY
32:   AFP/Getty Images
35:   S. M. Amin/Saudi Aramco World/PADIA
36:   Bildarchiv Preussischer Kulturbesitz/Art Resource, NY
39:   Victoria & Albert Museum, London/Art Resource, NY
40:   Archivo Iconografico, S.A./Corbis
45:   Charles and Josette Lenars/Corbis
48:   AFP/Getty Images
52:   Turkish Tourist Office

54:   Dick Doughty/Saudi Aramco World/PADIA
56:   William Tracy/Saudi Aramco World/PADIA
59:   Réunion des Musees Nationaux/Art Resource, NY
61:   SEF/Art Resource, NY
62:   John Feeney/Saudi Aramco World/PADIA
65:   Giraudon/Art Resource, NY
66:   Erich Lessing/Art Resource, NY
70:   Hulton/Archive/Getty Images
73:   Saudi Aramco World/PADIA
76:   Bettmann/Corbis
78:   Hulton/Archive/Getty Images
81:   Hulton/Archive/Getty Images
82:   Hulton/Archive/Getty Images
84:   PhotoDisc
88:   Tor Eigeland/Saudi Aramco World/PADIA
91:   Bettmann/Corbis
96:   used under license from Shutterstock, Inc.
99:   Shahreen / Shutterstock.com
100: S. M. Amin/Saudi Aramco World/PADIA
102: Hikrcn / Shutterstock.com
105: used under license from Shutterstock, Inc.
106: Anton Ivanov / Shutterstock.com

Contributors

Senior Consultant CAMILLE PECASTAING, PH.D., is acting director of the Middle East Studies Program at the Paul H. Nitze School of Advanced International Studies at Johns Hopkins University. A student of behavioral sciences and historical sociology, Dr. Pecastaing's research focuses on the cognitive and emotive foundations of xenophobic political cultures and ethnoreligious violence, using the Muslim world and its European and Asian peripheries as a case study. He has written on political Islam, Islamist terrorism, social change, and globalization. Pecastaing's essays have appeared in many journals, including World Affairs and Policy Review. He is the author of *Jihad in the Arabian Sea* (Hoover Institution Press, 2011).

General Editor DR. SHAMS INATI is a Professor of Islamic Studies at Villanova University. She is a specialist in Islamic philosophy and theology and has published widely in the field. Her publications include *Remarks and Admonitions, Part One: Logic* (1984), *Our Philosophy* (1987), *Ibn Sina and Mysticism* (1996), *The Second Republic of Lebanon* (1999), *The Problem of Evil: Ibn Sina's Theodicy* (2000), and *Iraq: Its History, People, and Politics* (2003). She has also written a large number of articles that have appeared in books, journals, and encyclopedias.

   Dr. Inati has been the recipient of a number of awards and honors, including an Andrew Mellon Fellowship, an Endowment for the Humanities grant, a U.S. Department of Defense grant, and a Fulbright grant. For further information about her work, see www.homepage.villanova.edu/shams.inati.

MUSHEER MANSOOR has written magazine and newspaper articles for young readers. This is his first book. He lives in Dearborn, Michigan, with his wife and their two children.